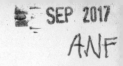
About the Authors

Donal Fallon is a historian and writer based in Dublin. His books include *The Pillar: The Life and Afterlife of the Nelson Pillar* (New Island, 2014) and a biography of Major John MacBride (O'Brien, 2015).

Sam McGrath completed the Archives and Record Management Masters course in UCD in 2013. He has since worked on projects with the National Library, the Heritage Council, the National Archives, Fingal County Council, U2 and the Joe Strummer Foundation.

Ciarán Murray is the only non-native of the CHTM! trio. Born and raised in Mullingar, he moved to Dublin in 2001 to pursue a degree in English and Philosophy and hasn't left since.

About the Authors

Donal Fallon is a historian and writer based in Dublin. His books include *The Pillar: The Life and Afterlife of the Nelson Pillar* (New Island, 2014) and a biography of *Seán MacDiarmada* (RIC, Banna, 2015).

Sam McGrath completed the Archives and Record Management Masters course in UCD in 2013. He has since worked on projects with the National Library, the Heritage Council, the National Archives, Fingal County Council, IT2 and the Joe Summers Foundation.

Ciaran Murray is the only non-native of the CHTM! club. Born and raised in Mullingar, he moved to Dublin in 2001 to pursue a degree in English and Philosophy and hasn't left since.

COME HERE TO ME!

DUBLIN'S OTHER HISTORY

Donal Fallon

Sam McGrath

Ciarán Murray

NEW ISLAND

COME HERE TO ME!
First published 2012
This edition published 2016
New Island Books
16 Priory Hall Office Park
Stillorgan
Co. Dublin
Republic of Ireland

www.newisland.ie

PRINT ISBN: 978-1-84840-580-6
EPUB ISBN: 978-1-84840-198-3
MOBI ISBN: 978-1-84840-199-0

British Library Cataloguing in Publication Data.
A CIP catalogue record for this book is available from the British Library.

Typeset by JVR Creative India
Cover design by Karen Vaughan
Cover image & illustration by Luke Fallon
Printed by TJ International Ltd, Padstow, Cornwall

10 9 8 7 6 5 4 3 2 1

Dedications

Donal
To my parents, for teaching me the value of history and culture, and to my brother Luke for his friendship and knowledge.

Sam
To my dear grandparents Peggy and Des.

Ciarán
To my late father, who instilled in me and everyone he met the virtue of common decency. My hero, always.

CHTM! Thanks

Eoin Purcell and all at New Island Books for having faith in us.

All readers of *Come Here To Me!* and in particular those who comment and engage with the site.

Those who contributed content to this book: Paul Reynolds, Luke Fallon, Mice Hell, Paul Duffy, Donal Mangan, Michael Costelloe, Matthew Lloyd, John Davies, Graham Hickey, Sebastian Dooris, and Mick Morgan.

Donal Thanks: Thank you to all family and friends for encouragement and support. Beir Bua.

Sam Thanks: My parents, all of my family and friends, and everyone who makes this city such an exciting place to live. Keep on keepin' on.

Ciaran Thanks: Donal and Sam without whom CHTM! would be nothing and I'd be lost. My friends and family, in particular my Ma – for bringing me into the world, for putting up with me, and for being you.

'This graveyard hides a million secrets,
And the trees know more than they can tell.
The ghosts of the saints and the scholars will haunt you,
In heaven and in hell ...
You're a history book which I never could write, Poetry in
paralysis, too deep to recite.
So dress yourself, bless yourself, you've won the fight, We're
gonna celebrate tonight.'

–Philip Chevron (The Radiators From Space)
'Song of the Faithful Departed' from *Ghostown*
(1979), Courtesy of Rockin' Music

Contents

1. Dublin's newsboys of old — 1
2. The Dublin cinema manager who became the only Irish prisoner of Dachau — 6
3. An unsolved mystery – the theft of the Irish Crown Jewels — 10
4. Downey's strike of Dun Laoghaire – the longest in world history — 14
5. The Siege of Connolly House, 1933 — 17
6. это Дублин! (This is Dublin!) — 20
7. Bubbles and the Dublin 1980s Mod scene — 24
8. John Mulgrave – the African Boy — 30
9. The Animal Gangs and the 'Battle of Tolka Park' — 34
10. Vladimir Lenin and the 'Rathmines Accent' — 39
11. Lions and unicorns — 43
12. The Murdering Lane – how apt! — 47
13. Some of Dublin's oldest graffiti — 49
14. Kevin Barry, JFK and Nelson's Pillar — 53
15. Dublin's original Punk venues — 58
16. When Dublin firemen rushed North — 62

17. El Classico has nothing on this 66
18. Thomas Read's: A missed opportunity 69
19. Jennie Wyse Power plaque, Henry Street 72
20. The Theatre Royal hippodrome 75
21. Swastikas and Nazi salutes in Deansgrange
    Cemetery 80
22. Cloch ós cionn cloiche 82
23. Laps around the Ambassador:
    Stop making sense 86
24. Dublin Mean Time 90
25. Dublin's oldest restaurant 92
26. 1940s guide books to Dublin:
    Two case studies 96
27. The bridges of Dublin City 102
28. Drug use in Dublin (1964–1972) 110
29. When Loyalists bombed O'Connell Street 118
30. Early days of stand-up comedy in Dublin 123
31. 'A Lunatic Fringe Element' at
    Richmond Park 127
32. Lady Justice, Dublin Castle 129
33. The mysterious case of Karl Schumann
    (a.k.a Ashley Shoeman) 131
34. Gordon Banks, World Cup winner
    and supersaint 133
35. The curious case of Robert C. and the
    bombing of the Spanish Cultural Institute 135
36. The famous Vonolel, Dublin's war horse 138
37. Stompin' George and The Magnet 141
38. Grangegorman Military Cemetery 147
39. Stein Opticians 151

40. Raising the red flag over the Rotunda, 1922   154
41. Looking back at The Blades   158
42. Buck Whaley and the Hellfire Club   165
43. Seán Treacy Street   170
44. Lenny Bruce's whirlwind trip to Dublin   175
45. The Free Peace Festival of 1978   179
46. No sex shops please, we're Irish!   183
47. The Viking – Dublin's first Gay pub?   188
48. The Bowl of Light   191
49. Dublin's shortest street   197
50. A Stout and Handy Man: Dan Donnelly   200
51. Paddy Clare: The man who took sabbatical to fight Franco   205
52. Flaunting censorship, Irish feminists and *Spare Rib* in Dublin   208
53. The dangerous pastime of swimming in the Liffey   214
54. UCD in Sudan   216
55. Dublin's oldest hotel   218
56. Marching to Dublin, Maynooth 1916   221
57. Favourite Dublin street name?   226
58. Swastika Laundry (1912–1987)   228
59. Original pirate material   231
60. May your love shine a light   236
61. A conversation with Philip Chevron   238
62. The forgotten Captain Ingram   244
63. When Bovril lit up College Green   248
64. The tragic death of Kathleen Wright, Trinity College Dublin   251
65. Little John & Dublin   256

66. A historic junction at Pearse Street   260
67. Dominic Behan, out of the shadow   263
68. The Oak Bar & Crane Lane   269
69. Prince Albert on College Green   271

Select Bibliography   273

1.

Dublin's newsboys
of old

The newspaper boys of the capital have entered its folk-lore, remembered as the lovable, shoeless, cheeky gurriers of a time past. In reality, the newsboys of Dublin were once a sizeable and precarious workingclass presence in the capital who, on various occasions in Dublin's past, found themselves the focus of charitable and political organisations, who saw them as a potentially dangerous underclass in some cases, or as youths in need of guidance.

From the paintings of Jack B. Yeats to the written words of James Joyce and Sean O'Casey, the newsboy of the early twentieth century often featured in depictions of life in the capital in the period. Yet while the streets of Dublin were their workplace, they enjoyed little job security in life, which could bring them into direct confrontation with newspaper owners. In August 1911, newsboys in the capital went on strike in opposition to the terms on which the *Evening Herald* was provided to them by the management of that paper. It was reported in the media that a crowd of boys gathered outside the offices of the paper on Middle Abbey Street, and 'as several vans were about to drive off with papers for the city newsagents shops, the boys surrounded them, threw stones and other missiles at the drivers, and then swarmed up the sides and pulled down the papers, which were ripped to shreds.' During the dispute there were reports of bundles of the *Herald* being thrown into the Liffey by youngsters in protest, and of the newsboys even organising their own rally at Beresford Place, in the style of trade union rallies common at the location. *The Irish Times* reported that following a meeting of several hundred youths there, the boys marched towards the offices of the *Evening Herald*, and that at the head of this procession was 'an imposing squad of youngsters decked out in the manner of Red Indians as they appear in lurid pictures illustrating tales of the Wild West.'

The newsboys enjoyed a good working relationship with the trade union movement at this point, and as Padraig Yeates has noted in his study of the 1913 Lockout, Jim Larkin had mobilised them. By organising these newsboys, Larkin had established a distribution network for the publications of the Labour movement in the city, crucially important during the events of 1913. Yeates has noted that boys took a higher commission from sales of the union paper than they did from the *Irish Independent*, controlled by William Martin Murphy. A sizeable number of Dublin newsboys would appear before the courts in 1913 on charges of intimidation against strike breakers, with tough sentences dealt out against the youths in many cases. Of course, the early twentieth century was a miserable period in Dublin's history, and as Joseph V. O'Brien noted in the classic *Dear, Dirty Dublin,* the pneumonia wards of Dublin's hospitals, at a time when a third of the city lived in slum conditions, held more than their fair share of newsboys and street traders. Their 'miserable physiques and ill-clad bodies' stood little chance against the elements.

It's ironic, given that the newsboys played a role in that great showdown between Jim Larkin and William Martin Murphy, that it would be a son of Murphy's, William Lombard Murphy, who would be among those attempting to reach out to the boys through charitable means. The Belvedere Newsboys' Club was to serve as a charitable organisation, which by 1928 was operating out of a location on Pearse Street. It had been founded a decade earlier by former students of Belvedere College with the aim of helping young newsboys in the area. At the opening of their Pearse Street premises, Murphy remarked that: 'Everyone who knows the Dublin newsboy knows what good qualities are to be found in him. He might not possess the greater civic virtues such as thrift and order and regularity, but he had immense loyalty to parents and an innate and essential decency of mind.' The Belvedere Newsboys' Club has evolved into today's Belvedere Youth Club, which boasts over 350 members. Gerry Walsh's excellent book *How'ya Doc?,* a study of the Newsboys' Club, is a great insight into a forgotten bit of working-class Dublin history.

The initial 'Animal Gang' of the 1930s emerged out of a dispute between the newsboys of the capital and republicans, who clashed over the wholesale cost of *An Phoblacht* during a 1934 printers strike. Demanding a cheaper rate, Garda reports note that dozens of newsboys attacked the distribution offices of the newspaper. They also attacked the offices of the Republican Congress organisation, again seeking a cheaper wholesale rate, and Gardaí noted that following their assault on Frank Ryan, who would later lead Irishmen to Spain to fight Franco, he informed them they were 'little better than animals'. This is the Garda theory put forward for the origins of the term 'Animal Gang' among young newsboys in Dublin. Interestingly, when the IRA sought out the newsboys responsible for attacking *An Phoblacht*, they went to a social hall where they were known to gather, which was the Ardee Hall on Talbot Street. It is clear from Garda reports there was a belief that a 'certain type' of youngster attended this club. It is evident that a sizeable percentage of young newsboys wished to mingle away from the influence of political and charitable organisations.

Today's labour laws of course mean that the newspaper boy of old is no longer to be seen on Dublin's streets. It is evidently clear from oral histories of the past that those who made their living on the streets held no romantic view of their situation. The difficulty of the lives faced by these children was perhaps best captured in the pages of *The Irish Times* in 1911 when the paper noted of the newsboy: 'He lives from day to day, and his failures and successes are reckoned ruthlessly in terms of food and lodging, or their absence.'

2.

The Dublin cinema manager who became the only Irish prisoner of Dachau

If you stand in the visitors centre in Dachau, you will see a large map of Europe on the wall. Over each country is a number, indicating how many of their citizens were imprisoned in the camp. The number '1' is marked over Ireland. This is the story of John McGrath, who became the only Irish prisoner of Dachau.

John McGrath (c. 1893–27 November 1946), was born in Elphin, Roscommon and educated at the Christian Brothers' Schools in Carrick-On-Shannon. Joining the British Army, he saw action in France in World War One.

Returning home safely, he worked as an administrative staff assistant at the Gordon Hotel in London and was involved with the organising of the Grand Prix Motor Race in the Phoenix Park and the Military Tattoo in Landsdowne Road in the late 1920s

He became the first House Manager of the new Savoy Cinema in Dublin in 1929, staying there for two years.

When the Savoy Cinema in Cork was opened, he was sent down to manage it and worked there for a further two years. Returning to Dublin, in 1935, to manage the Theatre Royal on Hawkins Street, McGrath was recalled to the British Army as Major at the outbreak of war in 1939.

Landing with the Allies in Dunkirk in May 1940, McGrath was one of the 'small Allied band' who fought in France after the evacuation. He was wounded twice in battle near Rouen, Normandy before finally being captured by the Nazis. McGrath, now a Colonel, along with other captured POWs were then forced to march over 400 miles to Germany. At least two hundred of the captured men died of exhaustion en route.

Brought to the Oflag (officers' camp) in Luckenwalde, he was imprisoned there for just under a year

McGrath was then transferred to the Friesack Camp, a special camp for Irishmen of the British Army. Here, the Irish were made various offers by the Nazis that in return for their freedom, they could become German agents and help sabotage the war effort in England, Germany and Scotland. 'These men', Col. McGrath said in a 1946 interview, 'were continually being interviewed in secret, and all kinds of proposals, including very lucrative offers, were made to them. In not one single case did the Germans succeed....'

After nine months of trying, the Germans gave up trying to 'turn' the 180 Irishmen in the camp.

McGrath was caught attempting to pass information about the camp to the Irish legislature in Rome, and so was sent to the infamous Sachsenhausen camp near Frankfurt.

On arrival he was 'stripped, searched and arrested by the Gestapo' and lodged in the prison section of the camp. For the next year, he was kept in near solitary confinement.

McGrath was transferred yet again, this time to the even more notorious Dachau concentration camp. One of the Nazis' first prison camps, it would claim the lives of over 30,000 prisoners.

Here, even 'important' prisoners like McGrath had their heads shaved, were forced to wear the striped camp uniform and were subject to regular beatings from the brutal SS guards.

For nearly two years, McGrath struggled and survived in the camp becoming its the first and only ever Irish inmate.

In the summer of 1945 with the U.S. 7th army sweeping through France and Germany, the SS marched the 'principal captives' of Dachau, which included McGrath, to Innsbruck and then to Tyrol in Austria.

There, lodged in a hotel that had been closed for six years, McGrath and 130 other people were locked away in the bitter cold with no little or no food, at which stage they were on the verge of death.

In an amazing turn of events, the U.S. army tracked the SS and the prisoners to Tyrol. Taking them completely by surprise, the U.S. took prisoner the 150 SS men who had guarded Dachau.

From captured documents, it was revealed that McGrath's party were not supposed to 'fall into the hands of the Allies alive'. He had survived death yet again.

The liberated prisoners were then 'speedily' driven to Verona and by plane to Naples. He was then finally brought back to Ireland via London.

A special reception, hosted by his employers in the Theatre Royal, in the Royal tea lounge, marked his arrival back to Dublin in June 1945.

After a couple of months of respite McGrath, now decorated with an Order of the British Empire (OBE), returned to his job as manager of the cinema on Hawkins Street.

Never fully recovering from the physical and psychological trauma of his imprisonment in Germany, McGrath passed away, in his house at 38 Merrion Square, in November 1946.

Though he was only in his early 50s, he had lived a truly remarkable life. Having fought in two world wars, Lt. Col. John McGrath then managed to survive in the brutal conditions of four different concentration camps. The last of these was Dachau, one of the most horrific prisons of the war.

3.

An unsolved mystery: The theft of the Irish Crown Jewels

The theft of the Irish Crown Jewels is a mystery that goes back over a century, and remains unsolved. The jewels were not the equivalent of the English Crown Jewels; rather the insignia of the Order of Saint Patrick, the British Order of Chivalry associated with Ireland, and they disappeared in June 1907.

The Order of Saint Patrick still exists today, although there has been no granting of its knighthood since 1936. The Queen remains the Sovereign of the Order, and the Ulster King of Arms, the position of the person entrusted with the safe keeping of the regalia, is still in place. Supposed to have been assembled from diamonds belonging to Queen Charlotte, the jewels were presented to the Order by King William IV in 1831.

The theft of the jewels occurred in 1907. They were last seen in the safe in which they were stored on June 11 of that year, with the theft not discovered until the third of July, three weeks later. Valued at $250,000 in an article in *The New York Times* at the time, the jewels were stolen from a safe located in the office of the Ulster King of Arms, in the shadow of what was then the detective headquarters of Dublin Castle. King Edward VII and Queen Alexandra were due to arrive in Dublin for the International Exhibition that month, and plans were afoot to knight Lord Castletown during their visit. The process would have required the regalia of the Order, and was postponed as a result of the theft. Although the King is said to have been considerably angered, the visit went ahead.

Blame for the theft has historically been laid on a number of suspects, with varying motives. A viceregal investigation into the theft in early 1908 leaves no doubt that, whether or not he stole the jewels, the blame for their theft lay with the then King of Arms, Arthur Vicars. Known to take the jewels from their safe on regular occasions, mainly when entertaining party guests, he is said to have more than once awoken from a drunken slumber with them around his neck.

Investigation into the theft showed that there was no forced entry to the safe, and that it was opened by a key (two of which existed, both held by Vicars), or at the very least, a copy of one. On two occasions prior to the discovery of the theft, a maid had reported to Vicars that the door to his office, and that of the strongroom in the office, were left unlocked. On both occasions, Vicars is alleged to have shrugged and failed to act on the information received.

Another avenue of investigation pointed the finger at Vicars' housemate at the time, Francis Shackleton, brother of polar explorer Ernest Shackleton. Francis, as well as his brother Ernest, were rumoured to be in great debt at the time of the robbery. Shackleton, who held office under Vicars, is rumoured to have hosted parties in the office where the jewels were kept, and an article in the *Gaelic American* accused him of 'nightly orgies' there. Although Shackleton wasn't in the country at the time of the theft, this line suggests that he planned the robbery, which was then committed by an accomplice. Vicars, in his last will and testament (having been shot by the IRA on 14 April 1921, accused of being an informer,) maintained his belief that it was Shackleton who stole the jewels, saying:

> I was made a scapegoat to save other departments responsible … they shielded the real culprit and thief Francis R. Shackleton (brother of the explorer who didn't reach the South Pole.)

Other theories suggest both that the jewels were stolen by unionists in order to derail home rule and by republicans in order to embarrass the occupying Crown forces. What is known, however, is that the jewels were never found.

In September 1931, a note was received by the authorities, written on expensive notepaper, stating that the Crown Jewels would be returned in return for a ransom. Despite being widely reported in the media, nothing ever came of the investigation. One legend tells that the jewels were stolen under order from King Edward VII, and these were later fashioned into a brooch worn by Queen Elizabeth II. Even up to the 1980s, investigations were ongoing, and a field was dug up in the Dublin Mountains in the light of information received from an ex-republican. Despite a number of days' hard labour, the search was to remain futile.

4.

Downey's strike of Dun Laoghaire – the longest in world history

Downey's pub, formerly of 108 Upper George's Street, Dun Laoghaire, has the dubious title of being host to the world's longest ever strike. It began in March 1939 and ended in November 1953, lasting a total of 14 years and eight months.

The trouble started when the unionised bar staff objected to a senior male assistant being let go and a non-unionised barmaid taking his place. The owner James Downey's response was, as apprentice Con Cusask remembers, to 'sack all of his staff and replace them all with non-union labour'.

In reaction, the Irish National Union of Vinters, Grocers and Allied Trades Assistants put a picket outside. Here on, from 10 a.m. to closing, they tramped up and down outside carrying their battered placard: 'Strike On at Downey's.'

After five years on the picket, Con Cusack left to find work elsewhere, and two years after that, Patrick Young (the barman dismissed) also found new employment.

Undeterred, the union continued to send picketers for the next seven years. In total, it is believed that they walked a total of 41,000 miles altogether.

The strike was featured in newspapers and periodicals from around the world including *Time* magazine. It was said that tourists used to go out of the way to visit the pub to see for themselves if the 'everlasting strike' was still going strong. (This prompted some to suggest that Downey was paying the strikers in order to attract the tourists!)

A fantastic story, retold by maritime historian Frank Forde, highlights the extent to which the story traveled around the world.

On 20 March 1943, the German U-boat U-638, commanded by Kapitänleutnant Heinrich Oskar Bernbeck stopped the *Irish Elm* ship. Rough seas prevented the *Elm's* crew from pulling their rowboat alongside the submarine to present their papers, so the interview was conducted by shouting. During the course of the conversation, the *Elm's* Chief Officer Patrick Hennessy gave Dún Laoghaire as his home address, which prompted Bernbeck to enquire whether 'the strike was still on in Downey's'.

On the anniversary of the start of the strike, 3 March, Downey would host a party in the pub. He also, allegedly, would often ring up the union to tell them if the picketers weren't there when he opened up.

Downey, a former boxer originally from Laois, died in May 1953 at the age of 79. The strike finally ended in November after an agreement was reached with the new owner. In July 1958 the premises was bought by Hugh Larkin, proprietor of the Royal Hotel in Arklow and Flynn's pub in D'Olier Street. It was put on sale again in April 1963 and bought in February 1964 by the Dublin supermarket company of W.H. Williams Ltd for a five-figure sum.

5.

The Siege of Connolly House, 1933

Over three nights in March 1933, a religious mob laid siege to Connolly House on Great Strand Street. Connolly House, located at number 64, was the home of the Revolutionary Workers Group at the time, and considered to be the home of the Communist movement in Dublin. The attack on the building, and other buildings associated with left-wing politics in the city, followed on from a particularly vicious sermon in the Pro Cathedral on 27 March.

Among the crowd in the Pro Cathedral on that night was Bob Doyle. Doyle had been born into Dublin's north inner city in 1916, and ironically would later go on to become a socialist himself, even fighting on the side of the left in the Spanish Civil War. He recalled being in the Pro Cathedral and hearing the Jesuit preacher tell the crowd that 'here in this holy Catholic city of Dublin, these vile creatures of Communism are within our midst.'

Anti-Communist feeling in Dublin had reached fever pitch by the 1930s, and the Saint Patrick's Anti-Communist League had been founded only weeks prior to the siege of Connolly House. Anti-Communism had been a feature of the build up to the Eucharistic Congress of 1932, with *The Irish Monthly*, a Catholic magazine of the period, using that event to inform readers that there was a coming confrontation between the two ideologies of Christianity and Communism in Ireland. In an article entitled 'The Coming Conflict: Catholicism Vs. Communism', Capt. T.W.C. Curd noted that:

> The times are not without their significance for Ireland. In this year of Congress, the eyes of the world are upon her – a Catholic nation with a Catholic government and the social encyclicals of Leo and Pius open books before them.

There was a belief that the slums of Dublin could provide fertile ground for Communism to develop in the city, and the political establishment availed of anti-Communist feeling among the masses for propaganda purposes on occasion, for example the infamous *Cumann na Gaedheal* election poster of 1932, which attempted to portray Fianna Fáil as a Communist organisation and showed a red flag superimposed on top of the national flag, encouraging voters to 'keep the red off our flag'.

Over three nights, beginning on 27 March 1933, Connolly House came under repeated attack by a mob. On the first night, this crowd numbered several hundred, but by the third night Gardaí estimated that it was in its thousands. Gardaí noted that among the crowd were 'a large percentage of respectably dressed young women.'

Five arrests were made on the night, with four involving members of the mob and the other involving Charlie Gilmore, a republican activist with the IRA who had taken part in the defence of the building and was arrested in possession of a firearm. Weeks after the assault, the Revolutionary Workers Group issued a response leaflet in which they spoke of 'pogromists' and 'Hitlerists' bearing responsibility for such attacks, and noted that James Connolly had had to face up to such 'mobs' in his day.

An internal Garda report from 1934 noted that Communists in Dublin faced a huge level of resistance from the Irish public, and that: 'The greatest difficulty of the Communist leaders in Dublin is to devise some way of putting Party propaganda before the public. The hostility of the general public has made it impossible to hold meetings or Communist demonstrations in the city.'

It is interesting to note those who attacked Connolly House to show their opposition to an ideology they saw as foreign and alien to them left a petrol can behind, bearing the letters 'B.P.', for British Petroleum!

6.

это Дублин!
(This is Dublin!)

This is Dublin, as you've not seen her before; with street names in Cyrillic text, this map was compiled by the USSR in the early 1970s. As astounding as it sounds, it is believed that during the Cold War the Soviet military had upwards of 40,000 cartographers and surveyors working on mapping the world in 1:200,000 scale, Europe in 1:100,000 and some cities, including Dublin, in 1:10,000.

Belfast was also covered in their mapping programme, but while that map took up one page, the Dublin map is spread over four. The sheer scale of the operation suggests their serious intention towards global dominance, and locations of strategic importance are all marked along with bridge heights, road widths, rivers, vegetation and climates; they weren't taking this operation lightly. Tram lines are even marked on this map (the lines down the middle of roads, with regular crossbars) even though they would have been decommissioned long before. The GPO, King's Inns on Constitution Hill, The Four Courts, Trinity College, the Old Parliament Building on College Green and the Royal College of Surgeons are all marked, along with Mountjoy Jail. Oddly enough, Leinster House and Dublin Castle go unnoticed.

Four of the locations, including the much maligned Royal College of Surgeons outpost, are marked for their strategic importance and were also occupied by the rebels in Easter Week. Who knows – if they extended the map out further, would they have marked Mount Street Bridge, Boland's Mills and the South Dublin Union? Maybe Joseph Mary Plunkett's plans weren't so outlandish; the sites marked for strategic importance then remain every bit as important for military planners now. Either that, or the Russians had some sympathetic members of the Workers' Party, or 'Stickies', on their payroll.

A map of Dublin created by the USSR during the Cold War.
(John, www.sovietmaps.com)

7.

Bubbles and the Dublin 1980s Mod scene

Little has been written about the Dublin Punk and New Wave scene of the late 1970s and early 1980s, next to nothing on the rockabilly revival scene and even less on the Mod Revival/Northern Soul scene of the 1980s. This is a small attempt to rectify this.

'Bubbles' was the most important and influential mod revival night in Dublin's history. Located in what is now the basement of the Temple Bar Hotel in Adair Lane, the night ran from 1981 to 1987 – the golden years of the Mod Revival scene in Dublin.

Starting as a weekly event (Wednesdays from 8 p.m. till 11.15 p.m.), it became twice a week (Wednesday and Sunday nights) to accommodate the growing subculture. The 11.15 p.m. curfew was to facilitate punters getting the last bus.

Admission price was £1.50 (or a pound if you were a member). The cloakroom was 20p and, if you could afford it, a coke was 50p. Alcohol was not on sale. This was, uniquely, an all-ages event. However, as Paul Davis, who organised a Bubbles reunion night in April

2010, remembers, this didn't stop a 'few enterprising lads' selling cans of beer at a couple of all-nighters. There was also one individual who did a 'lucrative trade' in pills.

At the start, the music policy was pure 1960s mod and soul with a dash of '79 revival. Original Trojan/ Studio One Ska also made an occasional appearance. As time went on, Northern Soul became a staple part of the Bubbles diet.

A funny anecdote relates to a number of TV theme songs that were played every week at Bubbles. The theme from *Joe 90* and *Hawaii 5-0* were longestablished tunes that were attached to the Northern Soul scene (for what particular reason I'm not quite sure.) The third song that was played every week was the *Match of the Day* melody. As Paul Davis explains; 'this was never regarded by anyone as northern soul, mod or anything like that, it was Noel's (the DJ) way of saying, that's your lot, it's over till next week.' Nevertheless, you still had 'newbies', who were on their first visit to Bubbles, thinking that the *Match of the Day* tune was also a Northern Soul cult classic and they'd get up and dance to it. The regulars saw it as a great (and often humorous) way to distinguish the posers from the genuine fans on their first visit.

Joe Moran recalls his first time in Bubbles:

I think it was the summer of 1984 when a friend of mine gave me a Motown LP. I had just turned Mod and for me I just couldn't fit the style with the post-'79 New Wave and angry Pop and was searching around for musical satisfaction …

So my summer exams finished and I had told my folks that I was going to this Disco (Bubbles) in town and that it finished at 11.30 etc. etc., you know how it was when you're young.

So with trepidation we head into town and down the lane and up to the doors where we are greeted by some bouncers all dressed up …

Down the stairs and pay in and then through the arch and I'm there …

I note a crew of Faces and realise that I recognise one of them and he wanders over and chats to me for a while and I'm introduced as a 'friend of ours' its like the Mafia – I'm in.

The slow set is fading out and the crowd start to walk back down the tunnel past the jacks then I feel my heart start to throb as a bass-line attacks me from the speakers. A tambourine kicks in and then some falsetto harmonising rounds out the sound 'Before, I go forever, be sure of what you say', and then it sounds like the place is collapsing and there are people leaping over each other to get to the dance floor and the place goes mental. I'm looking at Jimmy Mulvaney (I found out his name later) doing what can only be described as the most spectacular dancing I had seen up to that point in my life. He looks almost like a mod with his neat hair, Fred and bowling shoes but his trousers are a little too wide and they flap as he kicks his leg high in the air and pirouettes and stops dead on the beat and then he's off again doing some more footwork.

I'm stunned – I look around and Ragger and the guys are laughing and joking as if there's nothing happening – I'm in awe. I had never had a song grip me like that with its raw power, its beat and pure exuberance.

'Ragger – what the fuck is that song?' 'Frankie Valli – The Night' 'Where do I get one?' 'Ah ask the soul boys when they are finished dancing – they'll get you one, probably cost you about 2 or 3 quid'

The floor is jammed with bodies, slim tall mods, cigarettes in their hands doing a variation of the block, bobbed black-haired girls doing this dainty stepping dance and the soul boys moving around the floor like manic spinning tops

The song finishes and the next tune on the decks is as fast and as hard-hitting as the previous.'

Bubbles closed in early 1987 after the owners didn't renew the lease on the venue. It moved to new premises in Abraxis on Sackville Lane beside Cleary's but many saw this as the beginning of the end for the Mod scene in Dublin. Davis remembers that the venue didn't suit us: 'it was a bit too trendy and bright'. By 1987, the Mod scene was dying a death. In the UK, the scene 'had already gone way underground', while in Dublin it was on its last legs.

Karl Carey (42) looks back on Bubbles fondly:

My first time at Bubbles was late September 1984. I was 16. Suits, Parkas, Loafers, Fred Perry's, Scooters and oh yeah, girls! My mod music was based around the 79 sounds, Bubbles introduced me to new mod sounds – Northern Soul (yeah I still have to explain what it is to people). As I get older I prefer to keep it my treasured secret.

Every Wednesday and then also every Sunday night I couldn't miss Bubbles. To be honest, some nights were just ok but when they were good WOW! The all-nighters were ours and ours alone, don't think any other scene had or has anything like it. Met the most wonderful people at Bubbles and even got the most gorgeous girlfriend and then wife because of Bubbles.

25 years, 2 sons and 6 scooters later I find myself getting more and more back into the scene … Some things have changed and I realise you can't hold on to everything you might want, but your memories will last forever….

After Bubbles, Joe Moran, Eamonn Flavin and Mark Byrne set up the This Is It Soul Club in the basement of The Plough on Abbey Street which then moved on to The Fox & Pheasant on Great Strand Street, close to Capel Street Bridge. This shared alternate Fridays with the Night Owl Soul Club, which Paul Davis ran with Stuart Chaney and Mick Duffy. Both clubs ran for less than a year. The early 1990s saw most of the original Dublin Mods pack up and move to London.

There wasn't another regular club in Dublin until the Dublin Soul Club was set up in 1995 by Paul Davis, John Dunne and Ray O'Reilly. Their night ran for six successful years in The Plough.

The Sleepless Nights Soul Club took up the torch in 2002 and the scene has been burning bright since. They celebrated their tenth anniversary in style with a packed out gig in the basement of La Fayette's on Westmoreland Street in April 2012.

8.

John Mulgrave – the African Boy

Saint Werburgh's Church on Werburgh Street is a magnificent Dublin building, both in terms of its exterior and its fine interior. In 1715, Commissioners were appointed for the rebuilding of the church, and none other than Surveyor-General Thomas de Burgh was to be the architect to oversee construction of the new church. Thomas de Burgh was an architect of great importance in the capital's history, responsible for example for the Custom House of 1707, along with the library of Trinity College Dublin and Dr Steevens' Hospital. It's a tragedy that the church where Jonathan Swift was baptised and Lord Edward Fitzgerald's remains are found has fallen into a sad state in places. In a 2009 article in *The Irish Times*, the Very Rev. Derek Dunne noted that the once glorious church had 'been neglected for decades' and that 'Saint Werburgh's is not ours; it is in the ownership of Dublin. The work needs to be done, it is almost too late.'

The church walls boast many historic plaques of interest, but one that caught my attention was dedicated to John Mulgrave, 'The African Boy'. A small, unusual plaque from the 1830s connects the church to a young boy shipwrecked upon a Spanish slave ship off the coast of Jamaica.

The story is that a young African boy was shipwrecked in a Spanish slave ship on the Jamaican coast in 1833, and that he was taken under the protection of Constantine Henry Phipp, the Earl of Mulgrave, Governor of the island of Jamaica, who went on to become the Lord Lieutenant of Ireland from 1835. When the Earl of Mulgrave was appointed to his position in Jamaica, he urged new measures aimed at better treatment of the slaves, which was met by resistance from local politicians. The British Parliament, however, passed the Abolition Act in August 1833, and as a result all slave children under the age of six were to be set free. In a speech delivered in August 1834 at a dinner to celebrate the Abolition Act, the Earl noted that:

> The embodied will of a mighty nation, enforcing the irresistible dictates of justice, humanity, and religion, achieved the abolition of slavery, and has enabled me now with pride and with pleasure, to join heartily with my Hon. Friend in the expression of our wishes for the health and happiness of the 'emancipated Negro.'

When the Earl of Mulgrave came to Ireland, his adopted youngster came with him. Mulgrave's appointment to the position of Lord Lieutenant was welcomed by

Daniel O'Connell. Charles O'Mahony has noted in his history of the Viceroys of Ireland that:

> The fatal weakness of Lord Mulgrave was his partisanship. He could look at nothing except through the spectacles of well-grounded opinions of his own. At a time when he should have exercised discretion, he rushed into the arms of the Catholic party, and thereby mortally offended the Orangemen and their not-to-bedespised co-religionists.

The plaque tells us that the young boy resided with the family of the Earl until 'it pleased God to remove him from this life by a severe attack of Small Pox' in February 1838. A picture of the Earl and 'The African Boy' sits nearby, telling us he was buried at Saint Werburgh's Church on the day following his death on 28 February 1838. The plaque notes that the youngster was a servant, and that his 'integrity, fidelity and kind and amiable qualities had endeared him to all his fellow servants'.

9.

The Animal Gangs and the Battle of Tolka Park

Writing in 1943 for *The Bell* magazine, the anonymous 'Crime Reporter' was tasked with detailing the violent underbelly of gang violence in Dublin. Unsurprisingly, he chose to focus on the 'Animal Gangs', who were prone to appearing in the pages of the national media.

He described seeing such a gang once coming down Moore Street, and noted that: 'They were all hatless, age 15 to 25, some with overcoats swinging open', and went on to write that 'they kept together in a sort of huddle, from which the ends of the first rank projected like wings.' The origins of the term 'Animal Gang' are unclear, with many saying they were christened 'Animals' owing to their behaviour, with Garda reports from 1934 suggesting Frank Ryan may have accidentally christened the first such gang following an assault upon him by newsboys.

The first Animal Gang consisted mainly of newsboys, and emerged out of the area around Corporation Buildings at the time of a 1934 printers dispute, which saw them come into direct conflict with the IRA.

The roots of the confrontation between this gang and republicans were not political, however, but purely economic, clashing over the wholesale costs of papers like *An Phoblacht*. Some, including veteran socialists like Bob Doyle and Charlie Gilmore, insisted, however, that a right-wing 'Animal Gang' had fought the left in the 1930s.

By the 1940s the term 'Animal Gang' was used very broadly, applied to most street corner gangs and appearing frequently in the national media. These gangs gave inner-city youths a sense of pride and identity, and as Kevin Kearns has noted in his wonderful book *Dublin Tenement Life*, some gangs deteriorated into criminal activity such as racketeering.

Two particular outbreaks of gang violence at Baldoyle and Tolka Park in the early 1940s saw a very serious crackdown from the state against 'gang culture' in the city at the time, with the first showdown at Baldoyle in May of 1940 displacing the Second World War from the top of the national media and whipping up hysteria in the capital that the 'Animal Gangs' were still alive and well.

The Battle of Tolka Park in March of 1942 that followed it was remarkable in its own right, an event that would see the national media reporting on 26 March of nine youths being charged with attempted murder.

'Dublin Football Venue Onslaught!' read the headlines of *The Irish Times* on 24 March, reporting on bizarre scenes of violence in the capital. Two days previously, during a clash between Mountain View and Saint Stephen's United in the Junior Combination Cup, blood had been spilled on the terraces of a Dublin football ground.

The clashes had occurred between two rival gangs: the 'Stafford Street Gang' on one hand and the 'Ash Street Gang' on the other. How did two Dublin gangs come to find themselves inside Tolka Park during the clash? Newspaper reports noted that one gang had, rather incredibly, gained access by travelling down the River Tolka. As Bernard Neary noted in his biography *Lugs*, focusing on the career of Garda Jim Branigan, it was believed this gang 'had gained access by travelling down the Tolka River, heavily armed, on a makeshift raft, and scaled the walls'. The *Irish Press* newspaper would note that the gang climbed the partition from the riverside. The other gang had entered the ground as a result of a turnstile man leaving his stile, permitting easy access to the ground.

'Crime Reporter' in *The Bell,* writing only months after the carnage, wrote in a rather tongue-in-cheek manner about the use of boats, noting that: 'Boats were used on that occasion, to enable the attackers to make their entry on the scene in an unexpected, as well as spectacular manner. I am told the co-ordination between land and marine forces was very good indeed.'

It was ten minutes into the second half of play when the rival gangs would clash. The *Irish Press* reported a spectator at the game as noting it was 'like Hell let loose', and the paper noted that the violence occurred for something in the region of 15 minutes, leading to 200 spectators fleeing from the ground in panic. Arthur Smith, a linesman on the day, would note to the papers that he saw a man running with a sword and heard spectators in the crowd shout, Ash Street and Stafford Street. He also remarked that one man, bleeding from the head, was carried away from the violence behind the Drumcondra end goal and onto the field of play by players. The ref on the day, Michael Corcoran, would note that he immediately stopped the game upon seeing the panic in the stands and that the injured man carried onto the field of play was then taken to a dressing-room. Around 30 youths were involved in the disturbances.

The nine young men brought before the courts days after this violence ranged in age from 16 to 23. In June, five men would be convicted for their role in the violence. In the June court sittings, new information about the violence would come to light. In one report it was noted that the men in the dock were members of the Stafford Street Gang, and indeed the papers of the day noted that not a single member of either gang had paid for admission to Tolka Park on the day, as if that fact were in doubt! It was noted that the Stafford Street gang had been the aggressors, but that the violence had led to serious injuries on both sides, and almost resulted in death.

The sentences handed down to the men from both gangs were severe, but designed to send a clear message. Four members of the Ash Gang for example found themselves imprisoned for 18 months each as a result of their role in the fracas.

Gangs of working-class youths, divided on geographical lines, were a feature of Dublin life at the time of course. Yet as a result of physical clashes like those at Baldoyle and Tolka Park, the state would attempt to clamp down on such gangs through the courts and indeed through a more hands-on type of policing. Garda Jim Branigan, in the popular Dublin folk memory, is often said to have taken the battle to the 'Animal Gangs'. Branigan was crowned Leinster Heavyweight Champion boxer in 1937. He himself noted that this commanded a certain respect among the youth of Dublin, saying he was able to 'approach the Animals, search them and talk down to them without being assaulted or subjected to verbal abuse.' In reality, however, the gang culture in the city was not defeated in the 1940s, and carried on into subsequent decades.

10.

Vladimir Lenin and the 'Rathmines Accent'

Vladimir Lenin, the Russian revolutionary, spoke with a Dublin accent.

He did, at least, according to Roddy Connolly, son of James, who said in a 1976 *Irish Times* feature that Lenin, more specifically, had a 'Rathmines accent'. This was due to Lenin being taught English in London (c. 1902) by an 'Irish tutor, who had lived in Leinster Road'.

After this was repeated in *An Irishman's Diary* by Frank McNally early in 2011, a letter was sent to the paper by Dalton O'Ceallaigh. In it he discussed attending, in the late 1970s, a Dublin meeting organised by the Ireland-USSR Society at which Roddy Connolly spoke about his visit to the infant Soviet Union in the early 1920s. After the speech, there was a short silent film in which Roddy was shown walking across the square in front of the Winter Palace in what was then Petrograd and conversing with Lenin.

O'Ceallaigh made the point in his letter that 'there was no interpreter, so they were obviously speaking in a mutually comprehensible language'. After the film, Roddy himself stated that:

> After Lenin's death, the Russians, on researching his life, believed that when he was in London (he) had placed an advertisement in the *London Times* to the effect of 'if you help teach me English, I'll help teach you Russian', the person who replied being a 'Mac' somebody or other was thus a Scot. But Roddy said that, on the contrary, it must have been an Irishman.

The 1930 memoirs of Lenin's wife Nadezhda Krupskaya offer some indirect support for Connolly's claim:

> When we arrived in London we found we could not understand a thing, nor could anybody understand us [...] It amused Vladimir Ilyich, but at the same time put him on his mettle. He tackled English in earnest. We started going to all kinds of meetings, getting as close as we could to the speaker and carefully watching his mouth. We went fairly often to Hyde Park at the beginning. Speakers there harangue the strolling crowds on all kinds of subjects [...] We particularly liked one such speaker – he had an Irish accent, which we were better able to understand.

On a side note, what exactly is a Rathmines accent? Frank McNally suggests it was a forerunner to the Dart accent, which came to public attention first in the early 1990s. The earliest reference to such a thing that I could find is 1908. D.J. O'Donoghue, in a recollection piece in *The Irish Times* about George Bernard Shaw, spoke about how Shaw had 'possessed a "Rathmines accent", which he never entirely lost'.

Seán O'Casey's *The Plough and the Stars* (1926) contains a 'fashionably dressed, middle-aged, stout woman' character who speaks with the accent.

A 'Jokes Corner' from the *Irish Press* from 1936 had this to say:

> Mrs. Mulligan of Dublin, it seems, has been on a visit to London, where she was impressed by the places of refreshment. 'In Dubbilin' she says, 'the fish and chips shops are only in their infancy'. She speaks very highly of London, too, as the place where everybody has the Rathmines accent.

The Radio Correspondent of *The Irish Times* in 1946 suggested that the 'broad or moderately broad 'a' sound (is) a defect characteristic of that mincing, effeminate speech known in Dublin as the Rathmines accent and in Belfast as the Malone Road accent'.

Two years later, another explanation of the accent was given:

> Many of the Radio Eireann announcers are guilty of frequent lapses into the genteel, mincing manner of speaking known as the Rathmines accent. One announcer keeps referring to Pakistan as

'Pawkistan', several of them talk about 'fawther', [for 'father'] 'curless' for 'careless', and worst of all 'infearm' for 'infirm'.

It would seem people tried to use the 'Rathmines accent' to get into pubs, as illustrated by this 1942 news story:

The use of the Rathmines accent to gain admission to the licensed premises of Mr. Patrick Belton T.D. at Santry Co. Dublin was discussed by District Justice Reddin at Kilmainham yesterday, when he dismissed the summon against Mr. P. Belton for an alleged breach of the licensing laws and he fined a married woman from Santry 5/- for being illegally on the premises and a married man 5-/ for aiding and abetting her. It was stated in evidence that the man said they were from Rathmines.

Finally, John O'Doherty in a letter to *The Irish Times* early last year said that the 'genteel Rathmines accent was still common when I lived there in the 1960s [...] it was also known as an 'ORE and ORE' accent, as it was widely spoken in both Rathmines and Rathgar'.

11.

Lions and unicorns

While the bombing of iconic Dublin statues in the decades following independence is well documented, other attacks on the iconography of the city have largely been forgotten. The Royal Coat of Arms, in the form of the 'Lion and the Unicorn', which appeared in the stonework of many Dublin buildings, was also targeted by republicans. In the 1930s, following an explosion at Exchange Court targeting one such piece of symbolism, senior figures inside An Garda Síochanna called for the removal of the Royal Coat of Arms from public buildings in the interest of safety and security.

On 11 November 1937, militant republicans were responsible for an explosion at the building that was home to the Engineering Branch of the General Post Office at Exchange Court. The premises had once been home to 'G Division' of the Dublin Metropolitan Police, and it was at Exchange Court that Peader Clancy, Conor Clune and Dick McKee were to lose their lives on Bloody Sunday in 1920.

At half-six on a quiet November morning in 1937, an explosion destroyed the plaster cast of the Royal Coat of Arms, with *The Irish Times* reporting that:

The force of the explosion broke the plaster cast of the lion and the unicorn into pieces, blew a large hole in the wall of the building, and shattered hundreds of panes of glass in surrounding houses, shops and offices. Bricks and mortar were hurled into rooms of the premises, smashing furniture and damaging official documents.

Windows were broken at the Olympia Theatre, and even as far away as Parliament Street, by the force of the blast.

In the Garda report in the immediate aftermath of the explosion, Chief Superintendent Thomas Clarke noted that Garda intelligence believed republicans had been planning an attack on a symbolic target early in November of 1937, and that Gardaí were monitoring memorial statues, poppy depots and the Ex-Servicemen's Park. Clarke would write that:

It is the practice to have a Garda in uniform detailed to patrol a special beat in the vicinity of Cork Hill but there was no member available on the night of the 10th/11th for duty at this point owing to the other demands made on the available strength for protection of Poppy depots, memorial statues, halls etc.

It was noted that Gardaí believed the IRA were likely to cause an explosion at the Ex-Servicemen's Park, or at some other prominent centre, between the first and the eleventh of November, in the run up to Armistice Day. The Garda report would note that the removal of the Royal Escutcheon from buildings in the city under the control of the Board of Works should be considered, owing to the damage caused through such explosions and the risk to the civilian population. In May of 1937, the statue of King George II in Stephen's Green had been blown to pieces, and such attacks were undoubtedly seen as a very real threat.

Discussion around the Royal Coat of Arms and its presence on Dublin buildings continued into the following year. In a 1938 Garda report it was noted that if the Royal Coat of Arms could be removed from places 'without attracting press notice', such a policy should be considered.

The 1938 confidential Dublin Castle report, on the *Suggested Removal of the Royal Crest from Courthouse at Kilmainham,* noted that 'the protection of the buildings on which it is displayed cannot very well be effectively carried out.'

Inspector P. Killeen noted that in the case of the Kilmainham Courts, which display the Royal Coat of Arms to this day:

In view of the attitude adopted by a section of the population of this country to such emblems as this, and in view of the damage caused on several occasions within the last few years to statues and monuments associated with the British regime here, I think it should be advisable to have the emblem removed, and I suggest that representations should be made to the Office of Public Works to have this done. The removal of the object now may save a great deal of trouble to the Police later, and may also save the Rate Payers and perhaps lives of citizens.

The National Graves Association had spent some time calling on the 'Lion and the Unicorn' at Exchange Court to be replaced with a memorial plaque to the three republicans who lost their lives there on Bloody Sunday in 1920. Today, such a plaque exists right next to City Hall, where the Royal Coat of Arms had once gazed down on Dubliners. The Royal Coat of Arms can still be seen in several locations across the city, not only at the Kilmainham Courthouse but also at College Green on the Bank of Ireland (the historic Irish Parliament), at the top of Henrietta Street at the King's Inns and at the magnificent Custom House among other locations.

12.

The Murdering Lane – how apt!

Proposals often come in front of Dublin Corporation regarding changes to street names; not least on 3 January 1922, when a document was put forward that proposed wholesale changes to some of Dublin's best known thoroughfares. D'Olier Street, George's Street and Nassau Street were amongst those names in danger of being written out of Irish history. Luckily, the document was only partially passed and these names survived. One place name that skipped attention in that proposal, and funnily enough, given that the name invokes little but ire in most Irish people, is Cromwell's Quarters; a laneway consisting of 39 long steps connecting Bow Lane and James's Street in Dublin 8.

Aptly enough, considering its inspiration, recordings of the laneway can be traced back as far as 1603 in the *Calendar of Ancient Records of Dublin* where its entry read 'The Murd'ring Lane.' Around the end of the eighteenth century, 'The Murd'ring Lane' became 'Murdering Lane', and on 28 December 1876 a document was put to the City's Municipal Council recommending the names of both 'Murdering Lane' and nearby 'Cutthroat Lane' be changed to 'Cromwell's Quarters' and 'Roundhead Row.' When asked on what basis these new names should be carried, the proposer replied 'to preserve historical continuity.' The resolution was adopted and the names were changed!

A bone of contention this one; even though, when counted, the lane only has 39 steps, Cromwell's Quarters goes by the name 'the 40 Steps.' Bow Lane tradition says 'If the first step is your last step coming down, it truly must be your first step coming up,' somehow giving 40 steps! Tradition also dictates that a true 'Bow Laner' should always refuse to acknowledge the 'C' word as part of their address.

13.

Some of Dublin's oldest graffiti

I had always thought that the *No EEC* graffiti near my house, dating back to the early 1970s, was old. That's before I found out about the following.

The landing window of Dublin's oldest pub, The Brazen Head, boasts what is presumed to be the etching of a highwayman from 1726:

On a window in Trinity College's chapel a painter and 'glazier' from Galway etched his name and details

John Langan halted here, 7th August, 1726. (Ciaran Murray)

49

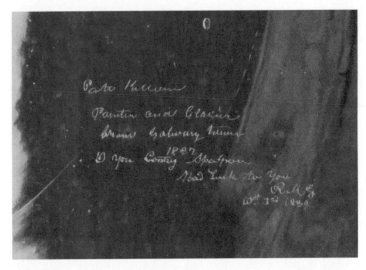

'Pat Killium Painter and Glazier from Galway town 1822 O you
Co[u]ntry Spalpeen Bad Luck to you Ruth G [?] Oct 3rd 1889'
(Graham Hickey)

'PB MOH RC 1924' (Paul Reynolds)

in 1882. Seven years later another individual, perhaps a spurned lover, let his feelings out on the same panel wishing bad luck on a 'country spalpeen' by the name of Ruth G., 'Spalpeen' being an old Irish word meaning rascal.

Finally, we have this graffiti from 1924, which more than likely shows three friends writing their initials on a wall on John Dillon Street.

A vintage Dublin postcard image showing the Nelson Pillar.
(Fallon Collection)

14.

Kevin Barry, JFK and Nelson's Pillar

Following Irish independence, the iconography of the capital became an issue of some contention, with debate on what should be done with monuments and statues relating to the British Empire. Perhaps no Dublin monument was quite as divisive as Nelson's Pillar, which stood in the centre of O'Connell Street from 1809. Writing in *The Irish Times* in November of 1955, William Fogarty of the National Students' Council remarked that 'the sooner we go ahead with the job of removing every symbol of British rule in Ireland, the sooner we can make Ireland, in fact, what she is of right – Queen of her own affairs.'

Fogarty was given a platform in the paper because the month beforehand a group of students from UCD had attempted to do away with Nelson. Their plan was ambitious. Having occupied the monument's stairwell and locked themselves inside, they proceeded to use what the newspapers described as 'flame guns' in their attempt to remove Admiral Nelson from his vantage point over Dublin. They draped a banner of Kevin Barry, the celebrated UCD student, over the monument.

While UCD students had failed to remove Nelson from his vantage point, the famous trade unionist Mike Quill attempted to do so in 1964 through more diplomatic means, by writing a letter in which his union offered to finance the removal of Admiral Nelson. Quill, a veteran of the Irish revolutionary period, had emigrated to New York and established the Transport Workers Union there, which included many Irish migrants among its membership.

In January 1964, Quill's union wrote to say they were willing 'cheerfully to finance the removal of Lord Nelson'. He made the offer in a letter to the Taoiseach, and it was responded to publicly by Sean Moore, then Lord Mayor of Dublin. *The Irish Times* reported the Lord Mayor as stating that the Corporation had no power to remove Nelson, as the monument was under the guardianship of trustees.

The Irish Times noted that Quill said his union would pay for the removal of Nelson from his pedestal and his transportation to Buckingham Palace, where he said Nelson was 'respected and loved for his many and victorious gallant battles on behalf of the British Crown.' Quill wrote that he believed the statue gave the impression to visitors, owing to its sheer scale, that to the Irish it meant what the Statue of Liberty meant to Americans. Quill suggested a statue of Patrick Pearse, James Connolly or Jim Larkin be placed on top of the pillar instead of Nelson. As a compromise, 'since there are two governments in Ireland today', Quill suggested President John F. Kennedy as a statue to place in the centre of O'Connell Street. Kennedy had been assassinated only months prior in November 1963, and discussions were under way regarding a potential monument for Kennedy in Ireland.

Quill noted that his union were willing to finance the removal of Admiral Nelson 'in a dignified manner and without hatred or rancour on the part of anybody.' The Lord Mayor of Dublin 'thanked Quill for his offer' though the city did not take him up on it.

The pillar, controversial as it was, brought something to Dublin in the form of the viewing platform on top of it. The monument consisted of a Doric column that rose 121 feet above the city, topped off by a statue of Admiral Nelson. The spire today is 398 feet in height, but unlike Nelson of course, offers no viewing platform. Immediately following Irish independence, focus turned to the issue of Nelson and whether or not he should be left as he was, next to the General Post Office. Its aesthetic value was another matter of contention, and W.B. Yeats famously said in the 1920s that 'it is not a beautiful object', but some prominent Dublin architects however, including Michael Scott who gave us the modern day Abbey Theatre, were insisting the very opposite in the media right up into the 1960s.

In the end, it would be a 'private sector' removal so to speak. While the state couldn't quite decide what to do with Nelson's Pillar, militant republicans could. The morning of 8 March 1966 was marked by a large explosion on O'Connell Street, and almost fifty years after the building opposite had been declared the 'Headquarters' of the Irish Republic, Nelson fell. The operation to remove Nelson from the street was, rather ingeniously, codenamed 'Operation Humpty Dumpty'.

While Nelson's head was among one of the few pieces of the monument to survive its traumatic experience, it would be stolen by a group of students from the National College of Art and Design less than a fortnight later. This was done to pay off Student Union debts. When one remembers the UCD students and their brazen attempt to remove Nelson, it was the second time in just over a decade Dublin's students had targeted Admiral Nelson. The students used the head to publicise a dance, and it was later smuggled to London. It ended up in a London antique shop, under the ownership of Mr Benny Gray.

In September of 1966, Gray arrived in Dublin on O'Connell Street atop a lorry, with the much sought after head alongside him. He was also joined, for the hell of it, by The Dubliners folk band. The Dubliners launched into 'Nelson's Return', a rewritten version of their popular smash hit 'Nelson's Farewell', composed at the time of the explosion. He inquired of a bemused crowd through a megaphone whether anyone among them was a trustee of the pillar who could accept the head, and a Corporation official came forward. Mr Gray said it was 'lots of fun' having the head in his shop, but the Corporation failed to see the funny side. A spokesperson made it clear the head was not to do any more travelling.

Bizarrely, in November of 1967, it was reported in the *Irish Independent* that the New Zealand cities of Nelson and Auckland were both interested in acquiring

The chart-topping single 'Nelson's Farewell' from Dublin folk band The Dubliners, just one of several hits inspired by the March explosion. (Fallon Collection)

Nelson's Pillar. All that remained at the time, however, was the head and some fragments! When asked where Nelson's head was, a Dublin Corporation worker told the paper 'we have it in safe custody. I am not disclosing its whereabouts. This is a closely guarded secret and that's because of the time it was stolen.' Today, it is on public display in Pearse Street Library.

15.

Dublin's original Punk venues

Continuing my research into the social history of Dublin youth subcultures in the 1970s and 1980s, I've tried to compile a comprehensive list of venues that were used for Punk and New Wave gigs from c. 1976–1984.

The main ones included:

- Baggot Inn (Baggot Street. Still there but unrecognisable.)
- Dandelion Market (Developed into St. Stephen's Green Shopping Centre.)
- Ivy Rooms (Parnell Street. Now Fibber Magees.)
- Magnet (Pearse Street. Renamed 'Widow Scallons' and then developed into a Spar.)
- McGonagles (South Anne Street. Demolished. Rebuilt and now Hackett London store.)
- Moran's Hotel (Talbot Street. Now O'Shea's Hotel.)
- Olympic Ballroom (Pleasant Street, Dublin 8. Closed but building still standing.)
- Project Arts Centre (East Essex Street. Temple Bar. Still in use.)
- SFX (Upper Sherrard Street. Demolished and developed into flats.)

- TCD Student Bar (Exam/Dining Hall?)
- Toners (Baggott Street. Still there.)
- Top Hat (Dun Laoghaire. Developed into Roller Disco, Fun Factory and now apartments)
- TV Club (Harcourt Street. Demolished (?) and developed into Garda HQ)
- UCD Student Bar. (Demolished.)
- Underground Bar (Now Club Lapello, Dame Street)

This blog post led to 110 comments! Some of the best included:

Niall (31 July 2011):

I remember loads of Skins used to go to the disco in St Brigids and then gave out hammerings to the Raheny/Clontarf hippies getting off the bus after drinking in The Plough & Flowing Tide.

The Blades headlined Lark in the Park, St Anne's 1983, over where the bandstand used to be [known as the place to get pot back then]. The Rhythm Kings supported. Huge crowd, think it was first ever Lark. It was the second version of The Blades, they blew everyone away, unbelievably powerful that day, fucking hammered it.

John Fisher (26 May 2010):

I saw Elvis Costello in the The Stella in Rathmines for his first Irish gig. He broke 3

---

strings in the encore but just kept thrashing away!! The Sportsman's Inn in Mount Merrion also put on loads of gigs. Bands I remember there include Desmond Dekker, The Radiators From Space, The Atrix etc. In Kevin St. Tech. College, I saw The Boomtown Rats & The Vipers. Most big gigs happened in the National Stadium on the SCR. Too many to list here but my faves include Chuck Berry, Horslips, Dr. Feelgood, B.B. King, Sonny Terry & Brownie McGhee, The Pogues, Elvis Costello.

Emmett (Feb 15 2011):

Has anyone mentioned the Top Hat, in Dun Laoghaire? Saw The Clash and The Jam there. During the Jam gig the back third of the venue was just full of people beating the shit out of each other … Oh, saw XTC play a big cabaret venue, down Talbot St direction, on the left. Tuxedo'd bouncers and Tommy The Bottle Of Milk ending up on top of a huge human pyramid in front of the stage. Also The Buzzcocks played in some club down Mary St way, you had to walk through a yard to get to it, I recall, or maybe I bunked in.

Eamon Delaney (Oct 26 2011):

I have a poster for the Punk Festival at St Anthony's hall 28/11/78. The full lineup, from the top, is the New Versions, Berlin, the Virgin

Prunes, the Strange Movements, the Skank Mooks and the Citizens. It was my first gig, and very memorable; a wild show, with fires being burned down the front of the stage as people set alight some reams of computer paper thrown around as part of the Prunes typically avant garde shock-art set. A woman in a wheelchair whirling around the moshpit, and kids from nearby Oliver Bond flats snook in to join the show. The Strange Movements had a single, Dancing in the Ghetto with Good Vibrations records and the New Versions had Regine Moylett as a singer, subsequently a long time PR person with U2. She and her sister Susan ran the famous No Romance punk and fashion bondage shop in the Dandelion.

16.

When Dublin firemen rushed North

The decision of Éamon de Valera's government to send emergency assistance to Belfast following the bombing of that city in April and early May of 1941 is a landmark moment in cross-border diplomatic relations. The response of the Dublin government to the urgent message from the War Room at Stormont was a remarkable moment owing to the historically tense relations between the two states. While hundreds of firemen from both Glasgow and Liverpool were dispatched, they could not reach Belfast until much later on the following day after the bombings of 15 April. Dublin's assistance was required urgently.

Immediately upon the Ministry of Public Security requesting the assistance of the Dublin Fire Brigade, men from the south would make the journey to the blitzed city of Belfast. From Dublin alone, three regular and three auxiliary engines would be sent. Dun Laoghaire, Drogheda and Dundalk each contributed an engine to the cross-border effort.

Writing in 1960, Dublin Fire Brigade District Officer Michael Rogers recalled that while the war had been raging for two years, 'it all seemed very remote to me. I looked on it as a deadly game being played in different fields and followed it with a fascinated curiosity.' No doubt such an attitude to the conflict was common. The Irish Sea, he noted, was his protecting moat. With the bombing of Belfast, all changed dramatically. 'Life had been lost and property damaged. My moat had been crossed.' Tragedy, District Officer Rogers noted, knows no border.

The Dublin Fire Brigade would make two crossborder journeys, the first on 16 April and again on 5 May. Following the first cross-border trip, the matter was debated at Dublin Corporation with Jim Larkin asking 'by whose authority had the fire brigade left the jurisdiction of Éire and proceed to the Six-Counties?' Another councillor responded to Larkin by enquiring that 'supposing Galway had been bombed, would any questions have arisen had the Fire Brigade gone down there?' Larkin insisted it would, and noted his enquires were in relation to payment of the men and also in relation to where liability would rest had one of the men been injured or died in the course of the cross-border assistance.

Fire Brigade historian Tom Geraghty noted in his study of the Dublin Fire Brigade that the response to the appeal for assistance within the job had been extremely positive. He noted that within a half hour of the message from the Ministry of Public Security being received, the Chief Officer of the Dublin brigade, Major Comerford, 'was addressing the Dublin firemen gathered from all stations at a meeting in Tara Street station.'

The first engine on the road to Belfast came from Dorset Street station, which was under Station Officer Edward Blake and 3rd Officer Richard Gorman. The Dublin Fire Brigade had first been contacted at 5.10 a.m. by the Ministry of Public Security, and by 7.30 a.m. three pumps with crews had already left the city. District Officer Rogers noted that 'Balbriggan, Drogheda and Dundalk slept peacefully as we sped northwards' and the men were greeted by customs officers on the border who waved them onwards.

The men were warmly welcomed to the city, with the *Irish Independent* of 18 April noting that 'the fire brigades which attended from Éire have been greatly praised for their work, and as they passed through the city's streets homeward bound after their errand of mercy they were heartily cheered by a grateful people.'

The first men from the Dublin Fire Brigade had arrived in the city just before 10 a.m., and the first engines departed the city before nightfall. While in Belfast, they had been exposed to a situation alien to Dubliners. District Officer Rogers recalled hearing an air raid siren during the course of the day, and recalled that 'I will never forget that wailing sound. From the roof top where I was standing the city looked so scarred and vulnerable.'

In the South, *The Irish Times* editorial of the following day noted that 'Yesterday for once the people of Ireland were united under the shadow of a national blow. Has it taken bursting bombs to remind the people of this little country that they have a common tradition, a common genus and a common home?' The *Sunday Independent* recorded on 20 April that Belfast was still burying her dead, and that praise for the southern fire brigades was unstinting in all corners of Belfast.

Men from the Irish capital would return to Belfast on 5 May, with even more men making the journey across the border. That time, six pumps and an ambulance from the capital would be among the southern appliances to cross the border. This assistance was not forgotten by the Belfast Fire Brigade, and when bombs rained down on Dublin itself in late May, it was reported by the *Irish Independent* that Belfast Fire Brigade approached Dublin to offer assistance if required. The Dublin Fire Brigade responded and thanked the Northern Irish fire-fighters for their kind offer.

17.

El Classico has nothing on this

El Classico. The Eternal Derby. The Old Firm. El Superclassico. In cities across the world, there is always one game that captures the imagination, the wits and emotions of the masses. From Rome to Liverpool, Glasgow to Buenos Aires, football fans wait tentatively for those days of the season where you meet your fiercest rivals; shaking in anticipation; that constant nervous feeling grips at your every bone. Sometimes it's pure fear, that sick feeling in the pit of your stomach – a dull ache that spreads into your chest the closer the time comes, culminating in chest pains and a dry throat on the day itself. Hoarse before the game even begins having spent the build-up yammering on to anyone who'll listen, whether they have an interest or not, about the game in question. Drunk on the occasion, not on the pints you swallow before it, you know you've got just a couple of hours before you're walking home with your head in the clouds or the gutter.

For the League of Ireland and Dublin it's no different. While, historically, Drumcondra versus Bohemians was the big one, and for all the 'competitive spirit' that a game between Bohemians and Shelbourne generates, there is but one game that evokes as much venom and passion as a derby should, and that is Bohemians versus Shamrock Rovers. The two teams dominate the history of the domestic game, (Rovers having won 17 leagues and 24 FAI cups, Bohemians 11 leagues and seven cups,) and their derby dates back to January 1915, when Bohemians took on Rovers in Dalymount Park in a Leinster Senior Cup game and came away three-nil victors.

For close to a century, results have swung back and forwards between the clubs, as their respective fortunes rose and fell. Rovers biggest league win over Bohemians was a seven-nil drubbing in Dalymount Park on the 5 February 1955. Bohemians have never beaten Rovers by more than four goals, winning scoring five but conceding one in 1929 and 1954, and beating them by four goals to nil for the first time on 29 June 2012. Between 20 October 1994 and that date, there wasn't much separating the two sides; they played each other 61 times, Bohemians winning on nineteen occasions, Rovers winning 22, with 20 draws. The highest cumulative score in the derby occurred in January 2001, when ten goals were scored in Santry Stadium where Rovers were temporarily residing. Trailing by four goals to one at half time, Bohemians returned in the second half and put five goals past shell-shocked Rovers, winning the game by six goals to four. The highest attendance at the game dates back to the FAI cup final of 1945 when 41,238 people watched Rovers beat Bohemians one-nil.

For all the stats and numbers, it's difficult to describe the emotions felt before, during, and after a derby game. For the victors, it's beaming smiles, unbeatable pride and cloud nine for all. For the vanquished, it's heartbreak; despair, anguish and sorrow. All the clichés, as hackneyed and annoying as they are, are completely true. Form does indeed go out the window on nights like these, and the bragging rights are more enjoyable than the points gained. There is generally a certain amicable respect shown between League of Ireland fans, but on derby day its all-out war. The Northside versus the Southside, the Clash of the Titans. Never mind your Anfield or Stadio Olympico; there's nowhere else to be on derby night than the steps of Tallaght Stadium or Dalymount Park.

18.

Thomas Read's: A missed opportunity

Thomas Read's, as the late and great Éamon MacThomáis noted in his book *Me Jewel and Darlin' Dublin*, 'was established in 1670, and are one of the oldest cutlers in the world'. It was the oldest shop in Dublin prior to its closure some years ago.

Its glorious wooden shopfront has fallen into serious decay in recent years, as can clearly be seen here. Thomas Read's shop produced cutlery and surgeons' instruments, and at one time was among the most respected sword makers in the business. Historically, the shop opened onto Crane Lane, but in 1766 this was to change with the opening of Parliament Street. Crane Lane acquired its name from the fact that before the magnificent Custom House of today was constructed further down the river, a crane would unload ships in this location, where an earlier Custom House stood. Parliament Street was born when Parliament gave a grant of £12,000 to build the new street, and the shop's address went from 3 Crane Lane to 4 Parliament Street, with its rear becoming its new shopfront. The construction of Parliament Street had been brought about thanks to the Wide Streets Commission, a body who would greatly alter the appearance and layout of Dublin for the better.

For many years, a licence dating back to the 1790s hung in the shop that read:

> Now we ... being two of the Commissioners of His Majesty's Revenue, do hereby authorise Thomas Read of No.4 Parliament Street, in the city of Dublin, cutler, to have and expose to sale at his dwelling house in Parliament Street aforesaid, the several articles hereinafter mentioned, that is to say, swords and halberds.

During one of his classic Dublin history television specials, Éamon MacThomáis visited the shop, and it was noted that the earliest reference to the Read business in Dublin dates back to the 1670s, and a sword maker by the name of Edward Read at Blind Quay. Blind Quay today is Lower Exchange Street. In 1750, the Read's business moved to Crane Lane.

The Thom's Street Directory of 1835 described the business as a supplier of 'surgical instruments to his Majesty', giving an idea of the prestige of the Read company. Changing customs would see Read's fall on hard times, and then-owner Jack Read Cowle told

The decaying shop front of Dublin's oldest store. (Donal Fallon)

a newspaper reporter in 1984 that while Dubliners always told him they were glad his business was still in existence, he would joke that 'you'd better make the most of me because I won't be here much longer.'

19.

Jennie Wyse Power plaque, Henry Street

On 21 Henry Street, a plaque that most Dubliners pass by unaware of marks the location where the Proclamation of the Irish Republic was signed just prior to the Easter Rising, by six of its seven signatories. the first few days of the insurrection, and following its collapse Jennie was active in campaigning around prisoners' rights and winning the release of those imprisoned for their role in the uprising. Jennie was a close friend of Countess Markievicz, who frequently wrote to her while imprisoned. In one example, the Countess wrote to her that 'I've such heaps of money nowadays. Jail is so economical!'

Jennie Wyse Power operated a restaurant and shop (The Irish Farm Produce Company) at 21 Henry Street. She lived above it. She was a veteran of the nationalist movement, having been involved with the Ladies Land League from 1881, when she was elected a committee member of that organisation. She was also a veteran of the women's movement, and a member of the Dublin Women's Suffrage Association, as well as being active with the Inghindhe na hÉireann (Daughters of Ireland) organisation from its conception.

Her Henry Street shop became a frequent meeting place for nationalists in Dublin, and it was above this premises that the proclamation was signed. The shop was used to feed rebels in the General Post Office for

Jennie Wyse Power took the Pro-Treaty side, uncommon within Cumann na mBan, and Cumann na Saoirse became the Pro-Treaty women's movement. It is noted in Cal McCarthy's account of Cumann na mBan, Cumann na mBan and the Irish Revolution, that in February 1923 the IRA attempted to burn down the restaurant on Henry Street, angered by the actions of Cumann na Saoirse (Or 'Cumann na Searchers' as members of the Anti-Treaty Cumann na mBan termed them). The irony in republicans attempting to burn the premises where the proclamation had been signed was clearly lost on some.

Cumann na mBan was the first national organisation to reject the Anglo-Irish Treaty. A resolution, put forward by Mary MacSwiney (sister of Terence MacSwiney, the Cork Lord Mayor who had died on hunger strike) explicitly stated that it called on… 'The Women of Ireland to support at the forthcoming elections only those candidates who stood true to the existing Republic proclaimed Easter Week, 1916.' This resolution was passed by 419 votes to 63. The feeling of the movement was clear.

Jennie Wyse Power became a Senator in the first Seanad of the Irish Free State. She pushed women's issues to the fore in this capacity. Interestingly, in light of her position on the Treaty, Wyse Power would later become a Senator with the Fianna Fáil party. Upon her

Henry Street plaque to Jennie Wyse Power. (Donal Fallon)

death in January 1941, she was buried in Glasnevin
Cemetery following a Mass at University Church, Saint
Stephen's Green.

20.

The Theatre Royal hippodrome

Historically, with regard to the theatres of Dublin, The Abbey takes centre stage. Its connection with Synge, Yeats and O'Casey and its association with the birth of the Irish Republic is unparalleled. Because of this it is sometimes easy to forget that there always has always been an abundance of other theatres in Dublin, not least the Gate, the Olympia and the Gaiety. For close to three centuries, the Royal seal of approval was granted to four different theatres in Dublin, allowing them to open under the name 'Theatre Royal Hippodrome.'

The first theatre royal was opened in 1662 by a man named John Ogilby and stood on the site of the modern Smock Alley theatre. It remained there, albeit in different guises (it was extensively revamped on a couple of occasions, once after the main gallery collapsed, killing three people) for 125 years before it closed its doors.

The second incarnation of the Theatre Royal opened on the corner of Hawkins Street and Poolbeg Street in 1820. Although this theatre attracted several high-profile acts, it never took off and burned to the ground in 1880. The theatre was rebuilt and reopened in the same spot in 1897 as the Theatre Royal and Winter Gardens, with a capacity of 2,300. Compare this to the Olympia on Dame Street, which holds 1,100 and you get some sense of its scale. The building was impressive, imposing and tantalisingly close to a direct view of its antithesis The Abbey, just 150 yards north as the crow flies, across the Liffey. Adorned with a stone columned palisade and a cast iron and glass canopy, the theatre was unrepentantly Royalist, and its posters often displayed the adage 'God Save the King!' amongst advertisements for 'Hammam Turkish Baths, Sackville Street' and the open daily 'Winter Gardens' serving 'teas, coffees and light refreshments', delights the vast majority of Dubliners at the time could only dream about.

More successful, and attractive to the elite, than its predecessors, this theatre was home to more than one good anecdote. King Edward VII attended a state performance here on 28 April 1904; not his first visit to Ireland. Edward had spent ten weeks on manoeuvres with the Grenadier Guards in the Curragh Camp in the summer of 1861. It was here he was rumoured to have been seduced by Irish actress Nellie Clifden, the scandal of which, it is said, contributed to his father Albert's death soon after. Charlie Chaplin also made an appearance here as a young actor in 1906 as part of an act called The Eight Lancashire Lads.

There was an attempt on the life of British Prime Minister Herbert Asquith whilst on the way here on

19 July 1912, and another attempt in the theatre itself on the same day. The actions were carried out, not by Irish revolutionaries, but by English Suffragettes. Their first attempt involved one woman throwing a hatchet at him as his carriage passed the GPO. While it missed him, it did succeed in striking nationalist leader and Home Rule advocate John Redmond. The second attempt involved three women who attempted to set fire to the theatre as the crowds were making their way to the exits after a performance.

The Irish Times report on the incident stated:

Sergeant Cooper, accompanied by his wife and Colour-Sergeant and Mrs Shea, was sitting in the dress circle of the theatre. About a quarter to nine, when the performance had concluded and the people were going out, he saw a flame in the back seat, just in front of the cinematograph box.

With the presence of mind that one should expect in a soldier, he rushed to the place, and found that the carpet was saturated with oil and ablaze. He and Colour-Sergeant Shea beat the fire out with their mackintoshes. Just as they had succeeded in this, under the seat there was an explosion, which filled the dress circle with smoke.

At this moment Sergeant Cooper saw a young woman standing near. She was lighting matches. Opening the door of the cinematograph box, she threw in a lighted match, and then tried to escape. But she was caught by Sergeant Cooper and held by him. She is stated to have then said: 'There will be a few more explosions in the second house. This is only the start of it'.

This incarnation of the theatre ran until 1934, when it was demolished and replaced by the fourth theatre, an art deco building that opened in 1935 and ran until 1962. Nothing remains of the Theatre Royal Hippodrome today. The site it formerly occupied is taken up by undoubtedly one of Dublin's ugliest buildings, Hawkins' House. There is now a housing scheme off Pearse Street named after the Winter Gardens.

There is a brief history of the theatre in Joseph V. O'Brien's *Dear Dirty Dublin: A City In Distress*. Published in 1982, this book also contains a great paragraph on the Gaelic League's denunciation of the demise of Irish culture 'as a product of the hegemony of imported English popular culture.' While in the early twentieth century, the Abbey Theatre put paid to the notion that Irish theatre was condemned to obscurity; the book also has a great quote from Patrick Pearse as he proclaimed the Dublin of his day held:

Nothing but Guinness porter. Her contribution to the world's civilisation.

Due in part to some of the works that have made their debuts in The Abbey Theatre, Dublin has proven itself to have contributed more than just Guinness porter to the world. Who knows how much more we could have contributed if sites of historical and cultural relevance such as the Theatre Royal and the Viking Settlement at Wood Quay not half a mile down the same side of the river weren't trampled on and replaced by drab, dour, and most importantly 'conventional' buildings?

21.

Swastikas and Nazi salutes in Deansgrange Cemetery

The 1947 funeral of 'Nazi master spy' Hermann Goertz at Deansgrange Cemetery, Dublin must have been a bizarre sight.

A crowd of 200 people, many wearing swastikas, bade farewell to the most successful of the Nazi spies who were active in Ireland during World War Two.

Much has been made of the major role that women played at the funeral. *The Irish Times* reported that it was women who wore 'most' of the swastika badges in the crowd, that it was a woman who placed a large swastika flag on the coffin and it was also a woman who whispered 'Heil, Hitler' and gave a Nazi salute just after the burial. The paper also noted cards on wreaths announced they were from 'Maisie', 'Mary' and 'My dearest friend – from Bridie'.

There can be no doubt that the 'Mary' and 'Bridie' were the Farrell Sisters from Glenegeary whom Goertz lived with up to his suicide.

Unmarried sisters Mary and Bride (a.k.a. Brigid or Bridie) Farrell (sometimes misspelled as O'Farrell) lived at 7 Spencer Villas in Glenageary, South Dublin. It was this address that Goertz gave when he was in the High Court in April 1947 fighting his deportation order.

Like the other women, such as Caitlín Brugha, Iseult Gonne, Mary Coffey, Helena Molony and Maise O'Mahony (another name on a wreath) who helped Goertz, it can be accepted that the Farrell sisters held anti-British and pro-Irish-republican sympathies.

Bridie was the girlfriend of Dun Laoghaire resident Patrick Moran, one of the 'Forgotten Ten' executed in March 1921. He was convicted of his alleged involvement in Bloody Sunday, protested his innocence and turned down the opportunity to escape from Kilmainham Jail with Ernie O'Malley believing it would be an admission of guilt and that it would let down those who had gave evidence on his behalf.

The Farrell sisters later owned a sweet shop in Dun Laoghaire and are still remembered by many of the town's older residents. Bridie died on 11 May 1966 at St Michael's Hospital. It is not known when her only sister Mary passed away.

In 1974, under the cover of darkness, a group of German ex-army officers exhumed Goertz's remains and re-interned them in the German War Cemetery in Glencree, Co. Wicklow where they remain to this day.

(Thanks to James Brady for information on Patrick Moran for this piece).

22.

Cloch ós cionn cloiche

It's a rare thing to come upon graffiti in Dublin City written in our native tongue. It's an even rarer thing to find such graffiti created by someone whose native tongue it isn't. On the corner of Rainsford Street and Crane Street, in the bowels of the Guinness brewery, is such a piece, and it's been there since 1984. It reads 'Stone after stone after fallen stone,' and beside this, its Irish translation '*Cloch ós cionn cloiche, ós cionn cloch leagtha.*'

It is the work of Lawrence Weiner, a conceptual artist born in the Bronx, New York and is one of a rare minority of his pieces that venture outside the English language. His mantra was that rather than creating a conceptual art piece, like say throwing a bucket of paint at a wall, you could, using typographic text, write 'a bucket of paint thrown at a wall' and it would do the same job. The best thing about this particular piece, though, is the story of how it came to be, told by Michael Costelloe, part of the crew who oversaw its installation as part of the ROSC84 International Art Exhibition in July 1984.

The English text: 'Stone after stone after fallen stone.'
(Ciarán Murray)

I was fortunate at the age of 17 to be part of the curatorial crew that hung the show. Lawrence Weiner arrived to oversee the installation of his work; like a lot of conceptual artists he didn't participate in the actual execution of the piece itself. I was assigned the task of helping the professional sign painter that was hired.

The poor man was afraid of heights and would have to have a 'wee drop' in order to have the courage to scale the scaffolding in the morning. With his direction (as he gripped the rail,) I painted the words on the brick. When the painting was almost done I remember the artist appearing below the scaffolding accompanied by the film director Jim Sheridan; they were in fine spirits. As Weiner was congratulating us on a job well done, Sheridan pointed out there was something wrong with the Gaelic wording. It was missing the 'i' in '*cloiche*.' The sign painter had left it out of the stencilling by mistake. The word would have to be erased in order for the letter to be reconfigured!

The painter flew down the ladder shouting that he was finished with the job as far as he was concerned and that it wasn't his fault that somebody had typed it up wrong. This started a swearing and shoving match with the artist; they both ended up rolling around the cobblestones.

The powers that be eventually intervened and stopped the wrestling match (which had become hilarious) and Sheridan suggested that maybe they should retire to the nearest pub and discuss the problem as gentlemen. The painter and artist readily agreed. Off they went. The original wording was produced and sure enough the word, as it painted on the wall, was missing the letter '*i*.' The paint was oil based and mostly still wet, so I went to work with paint thinner and rags and a scrubber and erased the letters (a faint discolouring of the bricks can still be seen.) I then realigned the lettering and imposed the missing '*i*'. You can see to this day that the top line is off centred.

The lads returned that evening singing songs, arm in arm, the best of friends … and everyone agreed it was a job well done!

23.

Laps around the Ambassador: Stop making sense

From all reports, the Lighthouse Cinema's showing of the outlandish Talking Heads concert film *Stop Making Sense* (1984) back in early 2012 was a huge success. We've heard reports about a dance floor organically emerging in front of the screen around half way through the show.

However, this was by no means the first time that this film has been shown in a Dublin cinema. In 1986, *Stop Making Sense* was shown every weekend night for nearly twenty weeks in The Ambassador Theatre.

Journalists, writers and music critics, such as Dave Fanning, Graham Linehan, Jim Carroll, Donald Clarke and Gerard Byrne, have all spoken of the significance of these last night showings.

Ciaran Carty in the *Sunday Independent* in March 1985 was the first journalist to write about the film showing and urged his readers not to *'miss it'* as it was 'only booked for a week'.

As far as I can work out, the film was shown on 9–14 March 1985 and then reappeared on 14 January 1986 where it played every Friday and Saturday night until May 1986.

Dave Fanning in *The Irish Times* in 1986 wrote that the film had the effect of 'transforming the Ambassador into a disco'.

Graham Linehan on his blog has admitted:

I went to see *Stop Making Sense* every week for about fifteen weeks during its run at the Ambassador cinema in Dublin. They had to hire bouncers to stop people dancing, and when David Byrne ran round the stage, we ran round the Ambassador. Ah, me.

Jim Carroll, writing in 2003, also remembers the 'couple of hundred party people' who used to 'run laps around … the cinema' whenever David Byrne did something similar.

Simon Judge mentioned in a recent *Le Cool* piece that 'bouncers were hired to curb the pogoing of the mental heads', while Gerard Byrne in *Frieze* magazine said that the 'madness … usually ended with police intervention'.

Donald Clarke, back in 2006, said the experience of these late night screenings was 'akin to actually seeing the band in action'.

Dave Fanning summed it up a few years ago when he said that this sold-out run of shows:

… provided one of the most memorable yet unsung highlights of the Irish rock decade and gave a whole new meaning to the phrase of 'dancing in the aisles'.

Things came full circle when David Byrne played The Ambassador, which had then been turned into a music venue, in July 2002.

CHTM! Comments

Ado Perry (16 May 2012):

'Amazing nights, on one occasion the film was stopped until the crowd stopped climbing onto each other's shoulders trying to make a pyramid. Great band as well.'

Ger Hughes (16 May 2012):

'Great memories of pub crawling up and down Grafton St. then staggering up O' Connell St. to The Ambassador, then watching Ton Ton Macoute (Sinead O'Connor) before the movie!!'

Philip Nolan (16 May 2012):

'I went about six times and would have gone more but I lived in the suburbs and there was no Nitelink then! I remember Dave Fanning marching up to the projectionist one night and demanding he turn the music up. When I was a guest on Dave's radio show a few years back to talk about my favourite album, it had to be

---

Stop Making Sense. I was a music writer with the *Herald* at the time and, as you can see, it almost became a club for those of us on the periphery of the music business, in radio and print media. I do remember a regular crowd and, yes, it always was more like a live gig than a late-night movie. Happy days indeed.'

24.

Dublin Mean Time

While it's often joked that we Irish are somewhat behind the times compared to our neighbours, it was once quite literally the case. Dublin Mean Time, which existed until the Time Act of October 1916 took effect, was 25 minutes behind Greenwich Mean Time. Once, Belfast was 1 minute and 21 seconds ahead of Dublin, while Cork lagged 11 minutes behind the capital! The Statutes (Definition of Time) Act, 1880, had extended Dublin Mean Time to the whole of the island, yet the difference between Dublin and Greenwich would remain until 1916.

Incredibly, prior to October 1916, there had been some hostility to the idea of synchronizing our watches with Britain. In August 1916, a letter appeared in the *Irish Independent* arguing against it on nationalist grounds! The writer noted that 'the question is whether we should give up this mark of our national identity to suit the convenience of shipping companies and a few travellers'.

The Time Act became a political football in Ireland, an Ireland changed (changed utterly you could say) by the events of Easter Week. Edward Carson, *The Irish Times* of 12 August noted, failed to understand the controversy of it all. 'All he could say was that if certain hon. members stopped this bill he would see that the Dublin Reconstruction Bill, or other bills, would also be treated as controversial and not allowed to proceed'.

Dunsink Observatory, near Finglas, controlled the time for Ireland. As such, Dublin Mean Time was sometimes known as 'Dunsink Time', and a number of prominent city centre clocks were connected by cable to the Observatory, in the form of the General Post Office, Trinity College, the Bank of Ireland on College Green and the Ballast Office next to O'Connell Bridge, which boasted a time ball which would fall every day at one. This time ball features in James Joyce's *Ulysses*, where we read: 'Timeball on the ballast office is down. Dunsink Time.'

25.

Dublin's oldest restaurant

Here's another good pub quiz question. What's the oldest restaurant, still operating, in Dublin City? I had a go trying to figure it out.

The following rules applied:

1) It had to be an actual restaurant, not a pub that serves food.

2) Restaurants within hotels don't count.

Beaufield Mews in Stillorgan seems to be acknowledged as Dublin's oldest restaurant (established 1950) that is still in the same premises. But what about the city centre?

Some contenders:

+ The Unicorn, 12B Merrion Court (Originally established in 1938 at 11 Merrion Row, it moved to Merrion Court in the early 1960s.)

+ The Trocadero, 4 Saint Andrew's Street (Established 1956)

+ Nico's, 53 Dame Street (Established 1964)

Trocadero restaurant on St Andrew's St. which opened in 1956.
(Source - Paul Reynolds)

+ The Lord Edward, 23 Christchurch Place (Established 1969, Closed 2015)

+ The Gigs Place, South Richmond Street (Established 1970, Closed 2012)

+ Captain America's, 44 Grafton Street (Established 1971)

+ Flanagan's, 61 Upper O'Connell Street (Established 1980)

+ The Lobster Pot, 9 Ballsbridge Terrace (Established 1980)

+ The Bad Ass Cafe, 9–10 Crown Alley (Established 1983)

+ Cornucopia, 19 Wicklow Street (Established 1986)

+ The Elephant and Castle, 18 Temple Bar (Established 1989)

CHTM! Comments

Mary Crawford (29 September 2010):

'I worked in Murph's during 1979/1980. Murph's was on Bachelor's Walk, with sister restaurants on Baggot Street and in Cork. The O'Driscoll brothers – Murph and Kevin – sold the restaurants in the early 1990s. They were very popular places, both for lunch and dinner, nice decor, good menu and pleasant staff (I would say that!). Main competitors were Capt America's, Solomon Grundy's (Suffolk St.), and a restaurant on Westomoreland St., the name I can't remember. It was 'Disco Days' in Dublin, a fun time, think we thought it was a bit of a Celtic Tiger, though we were all broke. Think a pint cost about 50p. Anyway, just showing my age, nice to think about 'the old days!"

Tom Tessier (March 21, 2012):

'I was a student at UCD '65-'68. The Manhattan would be packed after the pubs closed, especially Fri and Sat nights, most people eating eggs-chips-beans-sausage combos. Simple food, loud crowd, hot, full of energy – loved it. Tried Nico's once, because they had pizza on the menu. But it was a deep-dish variety, and terrible (maybe just a bad night for the chef, but I never went back). I went to the Paradiso a few times on Saturday night. Kind of genteel, well-upholstered.

A peaceful retreat, but I only remember that they served a great Knorr's oxtail soup. Another place that was popular for post-pub late eats was Charlie's, a basement restaurant on Lower Leeson St. They sold a lot of spaghetti, but I never had a good spaghetti in Dublin in the '60s.'

26.

1940s guide books to Dublin: Two case studies

Guide books to Dublin from the first half of the twentieth century have long fascinated me, and two in particular are worthy of mention, in the form of G. Ivan Morris' *In Dublin's Fair City* (London, 1947) and John Harvey's *Dublin: A Study In Environment* (London, 1949). Both are loaded with opinion, and in many ways are as damning as they are praising of the city.

G. Ivan Morris' book, the earlier of the two, is illustrated beautifully. The author was a Dublin publisher, who we're told:

> … in the midst of an unprecedented pressure of business, has taken the time to write this book for the guidance of visitors to Ireland.

We're told at the outset that the book is:

> … intended to represent an imaginary Dubliner who, in the casual way so typically Irish, is

showing his English friends around the city and neighbourhood of Dublin, and who, without any set order, is commenting on people, places and things as he meets them.'

On arrival in Ireland many of one's preconceived ideas will be shattered. The stage Irishman, who for years was Ireland's only advertisement abroad, will appear as he really is – a complete figment of the imagination of ignorant theatrical people.

G. Ivan Morris' book is clearly written by a man with a great love for the city, but also in places his frustrations with the Irish system and culture of the day are evident. He informs visitors that 'books by nearly every one of Ireland's leading writers are banned' and that 'if there is no free expression in a country, the cream of the writers usually leave it.' Religion and politics he notes 'are curiously blended in Ireland' and:

> ... the English are masters of tact and diplomacy, and, when they come to Ireland, they studiously avoid arguments about religion and politics, realising the Irish have deep feelings about these two subjects.

He notes that:

> ... another subject not too safe for discussion is Communism, which is most unpopular in Ireland,

Illustration from G. Ivan Morris' *In Dublin's Fair City*. (London, 1947)

as the church is strongly opposed to it. Despite this, there is a bookshop in Dublin specialising almost exclusively in Russian and Communistic literature.

Morris writes at length on the pubs of Dublin, and the pub culture and the changing role of the pub in Dublin life:

> … Since women have broken loose and invaded the bars and lounges, it is growing increasingly difficult to find a man's pub in Dublin where one may stand up to one's pint and tell stories without having to glance nervously around every few minutes to make sure that there are no ladies within earshot.

He singles out Davy Byrnes, The Palace and the Metropole on O'Connell Street, and notes that 'drink in Dublin is quite plentiful, and is only half the price it is in England.' The above quote dealing with women in pubs is interesting, but so is his remark that 'only in the poorer-class districts have the women been kept in the background' with regards to pub culture. The pub, he writes, is where 'the gravest political questions are thrashed out and settled.'

Unsurprisingly, Nelson's Pillar features in the study, and Morris writes that:

> Many people wonder why he is allowed to remain there, now that Ireland is free, but the general feeling is that the cost of taking down the Pillar would be out of all proportion to the kick the Dubliners would get out of it, and so it remains.

John Harvey's work, like that of Morris, doesn't shy away from sharing opinions as well as historical facts and information on sites of interest in Dublin. 'Nationalism is nonsense; but it can have indirect results which do make sense', he writes, as 'so far as Dublin is now both a flourishing and a promising city, it is the outcome of nationalism, building on the remains of an alien aristocratic regime.' Harvey doesn't shy away from attacking Irish nationalists on occasion, for example taking aim at the 'political hooligans' who destroyed John Van Nost's statue of George II inside Saint Stephen's Green.

Ireland, Harvey noted, suffered from an 'extremely thin-skinned moral censorship', a censorship 'so wide that the banning of books and cutting of films reaches a humorously fantastic point.'

Harvey is completely correct in his commentary on Dublin's ancient cathedrals, noting that they were both:

> … subjected to the horrors of well-meant 'restoration', which as usual destroyed the greater part of their original character and beauty. Both buildings were in a very dilapidated state, and urgently needed repair, but the work actually done was so extensive as to be even more disastrous than contemporary work at English churches.

Harvey writes of what he sees as the perception of the British people in Ireland, a rather damning indictment that '"The British" in many an Irish mouth has implications only equalled by those of *les boches* in France; it is one of the few sad instances where the Irish sense of humour is lost.'

Refreshingly for such a study, the tenement poverty of the inner-city features, with Harvey stressing that 'except for O'Connell Street and Parnell Street, practically the whole of the northern half of the eighteenth-century city is one enormous slum.'

Harvey's book is an enjoyable read, loaded with opinion on not only Dublin and Dubliners but also the political questions of the day, and the relationship between Ireland and Britain. Batsford, its publishers, produced a series on 'British Cities' in the style of Harvey's effort, and all contained the same style of maps and in excess of 100 images. We'll give the last word to Harvey:

To an Englishman Dublin has the virtues of a foreign capital without the drawbacks: artificial animosities have not annulled the kinship which has grown up through centuries of intermarriage between the peoples of the British Isles. Dublin seems to foreshadow the qualities of a new type of supra-national city; let us have a look at her.

27.

The bridges of Dublin City

The construction of the Liffey's latest bridge, connecting Marlborough Street and Hawkins Street, makes it 18 bridges spanning the river starting at Seán Heuston Bridge and working all the way along the Quays to the East-link Bridge at Dublin Port. The Ha'penny Bridge attracts the admiring glances of tourists, and O'Connell Bridge the traffic, but it is some of the others whose history or names give better stories.

- Sean Heuston Bridge (ex-King's Bridge, Sarsfield Bridge) 1829

The first incarnation of the bridge was built in 1828/9 and named Kings Bridge to commemorate George IV's visit to Dublin earlier that decade. After the declaration of the Free State in 1922, it was renamed Sarsfield Bridge, in memory of Patrick Sarsfield, leader of the Jacobite Rebellion of 1641. The bridge was again renamed in 1941, this time after Seán Heuston, a member of Na Fianna Éireann who played a prominent role in the Easter Rising.

At 25 years of age, Seán Heuston was Captain of a 23-strong company of men, mostly Na Fianna Éireann members around his own age, who were directed by James Connolly to take 'The Mendicity [Institute on Ushers Island] at all costs'. Their goal was to prevent British reinforcements coming into the city from the west, where the Curragh Camp lay. They held out until Wednesday afternoon, when they were scattered by the 10th Battalion of the Royal Dublin Fusiliers.

One of the more striking stories of the Rebellion is that of Lieutenant Gerald Aloysius Neilan of the 10th Battalion, who was shot and killed by a sniper from the Mendicity, while his brother Anthony Neilan took part in the Rising on the Rebel side. He was one of ten members of the 10th Battalion killed at the Mendicity, as per a report to Prime Minister Asquith by General Sir John Maxwell.

Seán Heuston was captured with 22 other men and executed by firing squad on 8 May 1916 in Kilmainham Jail. The charge was that he '… did take part in an armed rebellion and in the waging of wars against His Majesty the King, such act of being of such a nature as to be calculated to be prejudicial to the defence of the Realm and being done with the intention and for the purpose of assisting the enemy.' Kingsbridge Station was later renamed Heuston Station in his honour. The Bridge itself was reconstructed in 2003 and now carries the LUAS from Tallaght to the Point Depot.

- *Rory O'Moore Bridge, (ex- Victoria & Albert Bridge, Queen Victoria Bridge) Watling Street to Ellis Street, 1859 (Previous structures: 1670, 1704)*

Oh lives there the traitor who'd shrink from the strife, who would add to the length of his forfeited life. And his country, his kindred, his faith would abjure; No we'll strike for old Ireland and Rory O'Moore.

1641 to 1653 were particularly bloody years in Irish History. The Rebellion of '41, where an estimated 4,000 Protestant settlers were killed, and many thousands more were ejected from their homes, was the catalyst for the conquest of Ireland. This led to the death or exile of an estimated 25% of the Irish Catholic population. What had started as a *coup d'état* ended in the abject slaughter of a nation and the entry into Irish history of a wholly unforgettable figure: Oliver Cromwell. Little is known of O'Moore's personal exploits in the Rebellion, barring personal accounts and praise from other rebels.

The original wooden bridge on this site, built in 1670, was officially named Barrack Bridge. However, it became known locally as Bloody Bridge, after the deaths of rioting Ferrymen who tried to tear it down at its opening in an ill-fated attempt to protect their livelihoods. The timber bridge was replaced by a stone bridge in 1704, with an elaborate watch tower on the Northside of the bridge. That watch-tower was later removed, stone by stone, and rebuilt at the gates to the Royal Hospital, Kilmainham.

The bridge was replaced by the present structure in 1859 and opened as the Victoria & Albert Bridge. The bridge was renamed in 1939 after Rory O'Moore.

-*Mellows Bridge (ex- Mellowes Bridge, Queen's Bridge, Queen Maeve Bridge) Queen Street to Bridgefoot Street, 1768 (Previous structure: 1683)*

At around 250 years of age, Mellows Bridge is the oldest existing bridge across the Liffey. An initial bridge, funded by William Ellis, a rich landowner to the north of the Liffey with help from the Dublin Corporation (who paid £700 of the £6,000 it cost to build), stood on the spot for 80 years before being washed away in a storm in 1763. Ellis' family were also bound to maintain the bridge, and work on a replacement bridge started almost straight away, and in 1768, the bridge we see today was opened as Queen's Bridge. Another landmark to be renamed after the declaration of the Free State, Queen's Bridge became Queen Maeve's Bridge in 1922 (named after the mythological Irish Queen.) In 1942, the bridge was renamed Mellowes Bridge, and later Mellows Bridge, correcting the earlier misspelling of the name of Easter Rising veteran and leading Civil War protagonist Liam Mellows.

With written history of the 1916 Rising consigning activity outside of Dublin in Easter Week to references and footnotes, the efforts of the 'Fingal Battalion' in Ashbourne, Co. Meath and Liam Mellows' activity in Galway go largely uncelebrated. Liam Mellows was active in the IRB and Na Fianna Éireann and was a founder member of the Irish Volunteers. He was introduced to Socialism through James Connolly and it is reputed that the trade union organiser was deeply taken with the man, saying to his daughter Nora 'I have finally met a man.' In Easter Week he was given command of the Western Division, a troop of some 700 men. They were badly armed, with no rifles but a large number of shotguns, and provisions were hard to maintain as aborted attempts on the RIC barracks in Oranmore and Clarinbridge led to the Division occupying a field outside of Athenry. They were eventually scattered when British Cruiser Gloucester entered Galway Bay and reinforcements arrived. Mellows went on to play an important part in the Civil War, and was executed by pro-Treaty forces on 8 December 1922.

- Fr. Mathew Bridge (ex- Bridge of Dublin, Old Bridge, Whitworth Bridge) Church Street to Bridge Street Lower, 1818 (Previous structures: 1014, 1320, 1428)

While Mellows Bridge is the oldest bridge in the city, the site on which it stands only goes back as far as 1683. In the case of Fr. Mathew Bridge, there has been a crossing on this site since 1014, with evidence to suggest it was the site of a fording point long before that, and may be the original 'Ford of the Hurdles' after which 'Baile Atha Cliath' was named. The first reference to an actual bridge here, though, dates back to 1014, and may have been known as the Bridge of Dubhgall. The Bridge of Dubhgall lasted 300 years before being washed away, and another timber structure was built in 1320. This bridge lasted 60 years before another flood washed it away. In the 1400s the Dominicans commissioned another masonry-built bridge, intended as a permanent crossing. The bridge became known as Old Bridge and spanned four arches, with a tower at either end, with each side of the bridge lined with inns, stores, housing and a chapel. It was the site of the only bridge crossing the Liffey until 1674. The bridge lasted until 1818, when it was replaced by the current structure after the river bed on the north side subsided, causing irreparable damage to the structure.

The bridge was named Whitworth Bridge after the then Earl of Whitworth, Lord Lieutenant of Ireland, it was renamed after Father Theobald Mathew (the Apostle of Temperance) in 1938. Incidentally, two of the bridges over the Liffey deal with the subject of temperance, the other of course being Matt Talbot Bridge.

- O'Donovan Rossa Bridge (ex- Richmond Bridge, Ormond Bridge) Chancery Place to Winetavern Street, 1816 (Previous structures: 1682, 1684)

'The fools, the fools, the fools, they have left us our Fenian dead – And while Ireland holds these graves, Ireland unfree shall never be at peace.' The immortal words of Patrick Pearse, delivered at the grave of Jeremiah O'Donovan Rossa on 1 August 1915. For while O'Donovan Rossa was world renowned during his lifetime, raising funds in America for a bombing campaign on English soil, it was undoubtedly in death that he made the greatest contribution to the Republican cause.

Born to tenant farmers in Cork in 1831, Rossa founded an organisation called the 'Phoenix National and Literary Society' for the 'liberation of Ireland by force' in 1856, but it was membership of the Irish Republican Brotherhood, and alleged involvement in plotting the Fenian Rebellion of 1865, that caused him to be charged, without trial, of high treason and sentenced to penal servitude. Years of ill-treatment in British jails followed and he was eventually deported to America, where, from a base on Staten Island, he established the 'skirmishing fund.' The fund was hugely successful, earning $23,000 by 1877 and doubling the figure in that year alone. Though there was an alleged attempt on his life by a British Agent in 1885, he lived until 1915, when he died of old age. Aware of the political impact of the funeral of Terence Bellew McManus 50 years earlier and the positive propaganda it would generate, John Devoy and Thomas Clarke conspired with O'Donovan Rossa's wife, herself an ardent Fenian, to have his body sent home for burial. Almost 100,000 people attended the funeral at which Pearse made his famous ovation.

The Bridge itself was initially a wooden structure, built in 1682 under the instructions of Lord Mayor of Dublin, Lord Humphrey Jervis. The bridge was a ramshackle effort without even guard railings, and was washed downstream within two years of its creation. It was replaced in 1684 by a masonry bridge named

Ormond Bridge, which lasted until 1802 when it was swept away in a storm. After 11 years of debate, design and construction, the current bridge was opened, complete with sculptured heads on the keystones. The heads on the keystones represent Plenty, The Liffey herself, Industry, Commerce, Peace and Hibernia. It was opened as Richmond Bridge in honour of the then Lord Lieutenant of Ireland, the Duke of Richmond. In 1923 it was named after O'Donovan Rossa.

28.

Drug use in Dublin (1964–1972)

'Drug habit unlikely to grow here' read *The Irish Times* headline on 4 May 1964. However, while authorities quoted in the article may have held that optimistic viewpoint, the writer noted that the Gardaí had been keeping a special eye on a number of coffee houses in Dublin 'where it was suspected that "reefer" cigarettes and "purple hearts" were being distributed, particularly among students'.

Raifiu Ojikuto, a 26-year-old Nigerian medical student living at Pembroke Cottages, Ballsbridge was arrested in April 1964 for possession of Purple Hearts (amphetamine stimulant tablets), thus becoming the first person in state history to be arrested on drugs charges. He was found dead in his home by Gardaí after he failed to appear in the Dublin District Court. The death was not treated as suspicious.

In September of that year, a Glaswegian Stewart M. (21) and a Dubliner Colin F. (21) were up in court for drugs charges. The former was sentenced to six months' imprisonment for importing twenty packets of Indian hemp and supplying five packets to persons unknown on O'Connell Street. The latter was sentenced to six months' imprisonment on charges of being in possession of two packets of Indian hemp.

1965 also saw only two drugs charges.

In January, a 33-year-old Nigerian mechanic was caught with 10lb. 6oz. of cannabis in Dublin Airport en route from Lagos to London. He had no intention of trying to get rid of the drug in Ireland. In court, it was noted that Dublin had become 'a back entrance for smuggling drugs into England'.

Later that year in July, Julian R., 28-year-old medical student, was charged in with having in his possession 'a quantity of Indian hemp'. He was remanded on £100 independent bail.

In 1966, a 19-year-old student named Eugene C. became the subject of the only drugs offence case of that year. He was arrested by Gardaí on 30 April while in St Stephen's Green rolling a cigarette with Indian hemp. Pleading guilty to possession, he was fined a total of £20. The court heard that he had spent the afternoon with a friend in the New Amsterdam Café on South Anne St. This friend then went off with ten shillings to meet 'a fellow [who] had come to this country from England with a load of hash'.

There were no drugs charges in 1967. However, the year saw the establishment of the Garda Dublin Drugs Squad, which was led by the infamous Inspector Denis Mullins for 25 years.

'A young American living in Ireland' wrote a piece for *The Irish Times* (17 April 1967) in which he talked about the current drugs market in Ireland:

> I remember a dinner party in the west of Ireland where all the drink ran out early and all the guests, middle-aged professional people, turned to marijuana because the pubs were closed.
>
> The only convictions in Ireland under the Dangerous Drugs Act have been made in the last three years. There were only three, and for Indian hemp in the Dublin area. Heroin is rumouredly available for young people in Dublin, initially free, and increasingly expensive as addiction takes hold.

Things changed dramatically, however, after 1965. In 1968, 24 people were charged with drugs offences. By 1969, this number had risen to 59, and then 71 people by 1970. The increase in the amount of people being arrested for drugs offences illustrated the general increase in drug taking in Dublin as a whole. These early years could be probably seen as the 'innocent years' of illegal drug use in Dublin before the appearance of criminal gangs and large-scale heroin abuse that came in the late 1970s.

1968 also saw the first drugs busts. In January, Special Branch detectives raided several private houses in South Dublin and found heroin, LSD and marijuana. The raids were the accumulation of six months' detective work. At least six people were expected to appear in courts following the drugs seizures.

In January 1968, a UCD student wrote a letter to *Irish Times* journalist Michael Viney. He included it in an article published in the paper that month:

> I am an Irish UCD student. During midterm last year I went to London for a week and returned with 50 ampoules of Meth [Methedrine] strapped around my waist and also 2 ounces of Moroccan Hash [cannabis resin] and 2 ounces of West Indian pot.
>
> While I am writing this I am stoned on Meth – I've also started injecting it recently – and I have also just finished smoking a beautiful fat reefer joint. I also supply a number of my friends with what I've got. I'm not a pusher: I just like giving them experiences – make them happy. I've just shoved in that line so that you wouldn't think I was making money out of drugs.
>
> I don't know why I'm writing this – it's not a gag – I just feel so great I've got to write it down or tell someone. Right now I feel like turning the world on ... I know you've got to write about the evils of drugs etc. you should just try them sometime and write the article while you're stoned.

The Working Party on Drug Abuse (1971) stated that in September 1969 there were approximately

350 persons involved in the abuse of drugs in the Dublin area whose names were known to the Gardaí. By December 1970, this figure had grown to about 940.

By 1969, there were more and more reports of drugs being 'systematically stolen' from public health dispensaries while more imaginative drug users stole plants of Cannabis sativa from the National Botanic Garden in Glasnevin in October.

Larry Masterson, now a television producer in RTÉ, in his ground-breaking but unpublished study *A report on drug abuse in Dublin* (1970) mentioned that:

> During the summer of 1969, Skerries became a favourite weekend resort for drug users from Dublin and Northern Ireland (Belfast mainly) who used to congregate there on weekends in order to 'rave up' on drugs.

Masterson spent six months studying the Dublin drug scene, and noted that:

> The Bailey [was] one of about five pubs in Dublin which have become a 'meeting place' for drug users and where you can buy your drugs provided you are known and know who to ask.

Accompanying a drug dealer on his nightly trip around town, Masterson was brought to a 'Beat' go-go dance, and then to another well-known Dublin bar:

A sketch of the Hellfire Club's infamous Montpellier House on Montpellier Hill. (Paul Duffy)

'Apples an' noranges.' (Paul Duffy)

THE GREAT FIRE IN DUBLIN: RAFTERS CUTTING OFF THE WHISKY.

The 1875 whiskey fire, when Dublin was saved by Captain James Robert Ingram. (Dublin Fire Brigade Museum)

Gardaí inside Connolly House, Great Strand Street. The building was attacked by an anti-communist mob in 1933.

Crowd looking in at Oliver Sheppard's monument of Cuchullan at the General Post Office, Easter Week 2016. (Luke Fallon)

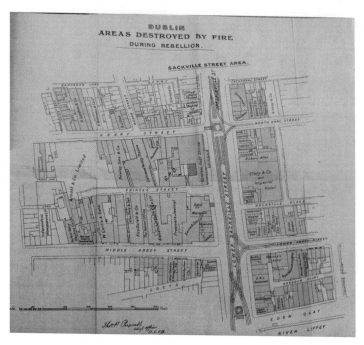

The destruction of Dublin. This map was drawn in the aftermath of Easter Week by Dublin Fire Brigade Chief Officer Thomas Purcell. (Dublin Fire Brigade Museum)

Mellows Bridge Plaque. (Ciarán Murray)

Postcard showing Dublin during the Easter Rising.
(Fallon Collection)

'There she stands, upon her station, with her face to the ground and her arse to the nation.' Lady Justice, Dublin Castle. (Ciarán Murray)

The Lion and the Unicorn, the royal coat of arms, once commonplace on public buildings in Dublin. (Donal Fallon)

THE RIOTER'S IDEAL.

'The Rioters Ideal'- a London *Punch* cartoon from the height of the 1913 Lockout in Dublin. (Fallon Collection)

A sketch of bareknuckle pugilist, Sir Dan Donnelly.
(Paul Duffy)

Two wartime Dublin Fire Brigade firefighters,
Jack Conroy and Dan Dowd. (Las Fallon)

An illustration of a Dublin newsboy (Luke Fallon).

Peter, who has been an *Evening Herald* street seller for over thirty years, enjoys a pint. (Janer)

Earl Roberts sits upon his beloved Vonolel. (Navy and Army Illustrated, Fallon Collection)

Brendan Behan reflects. (Paul Reynolds)

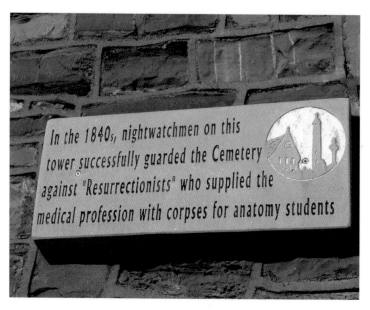

In the 1840s, nightwatchmen on this tower successfully guarded the Cemetery against "Resurrectionists" who supplied the medical profession with corpses for anatomy students

Plaque dedicated to Night watchmen in Glasnevin Cemetery (Ciarán Murray)

A mobile flowerbed, Bow Lane.
(Ciarán Murray)

Red sky at night.
(Ciarán Murray)

At the Jim Larkin monument during a 1913 commemoration in Dublin. (Paul Reynolds)

A reminder of the once thriving cattle market, Hanlon's Corner. (Luke Fallon)

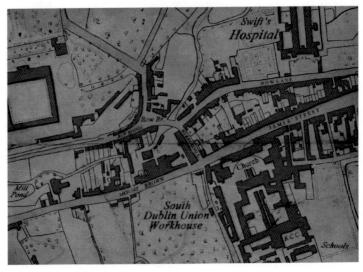

At the centre of the centre of the image stands 'Murdering L', now Cromwell's Quarters. (Donal Mangan)

Graffiti from the Tivoli Theatre carpark. (Ciarán Murray)

The Theatre Royal, Hawkins' Street. (Donal Mangan)

Illustration of legendary Dublin musician Philip Chevron
under Under Clery's Clock.
(Mice Hell)

[We] left the Checkmate Club and headed down to McDaid's pub where we sold hash to five more people. These were much older (20-25 years) and members of the 'literary set' who frequent McDaid's.

1970 saw the first seizures of homemade LSD, and Conor Brady in *The Irish Times* reported how the drug was 'gaining ground in the Dublin drugs market', especially as supplies of 'Lebanese marijuana were virtually cut off' to Ireland as a result of a Drug Squad investigation the previous July.

The following year saw yet another increase in drugs charges, and the first publication of a major government report, entitled *Report of Working Party on Drug Abuse*, on the use of drugs in the country. The 78-page document was drawn up by a committee of 18 people including doctors, social workers, psychiatrists, university professors, student leaders and Gardaí. Also in 1971, Garda Des O'Reilly said in court that people 'could get cannabis in the city centre as easily as chocolate'

1972 was another year of firsts when it came to drug use in the capital. In March, the police used a trained dog in a drugs case for the first time. Mack, the Drug Squad dog, found two small packages of cannabis in a flat in Dun Laoghaire. The year also saw the first major raid on a college when in June six people were questioned, two being charged, after the drugs squad raided the Junior Common Room in Trinity College and found a 'fairly substantial' amount of LSD.

In November, the first substantial raid took place on a house party. More than 50 people were questioned after a raid, in which cannabis and other drugs were found, at a party in a private house in Ranelagh. November 1972 also saw the biggest drugs raid until that time when 36 police led a bust on the Yeoman Inn on South King Street that saw a hundred people being searched, of whom 34 were arrested and 21 charged. The raid, which took place at 9 p.m. on a Saturday night, came about after detectives had kept the premises under surveillance day and night for 14 days. It was believed by both the police and the public that the pub was a popular place to both score and take illegal drugs.

Cannabis, marijuana and LSD were found littered on the ground, dropped by punters when they realised what was going on, while drugs were also found hidden in the toilets, behind piping or wooden beams and in dustbins. The narcotics detectives told journalists that after the 'lightning crackdown' they expected the drugs scene in the city would be 'become very quiet'.

The 1970s saw a general increase in illegal drug use in Dublin. 1977 saw 381 people facing charges for drugs-related offences, and by 1979 it has risen to 594, as was noted by Padraig Yeates in a 1992 *Irish Times* article.

This immediate period then saw a seismic shift in drug use. Coinciding with the fall of the Shah of Iran in 1979, and the resulting flood of heroin into Western

Europe, Dublin's criminal gangs, most notably the Dunne family, switched from armed robbery to heroin distribution. That was when the next, darker and more tragic, chapter of Dublin's drugs history began.

29.

When Loyalists bombed O'Connell Street

The Daniel O'Connell statue on O'Connell Street is undoubtedly the grandest statue in the centre of Dublin, commemorating 'The Liberator' O'Connell and standing at the top of what was once Sackville Street in a Dublin that is gone. The statue of O'Connell himself dates to 1882, the work of John Henry Foley, and boasts some revolutionary bullet holes on close inspection.

On the day of the laying of the foundation stone in 1864, the Lord Mayor of Dublin, Peter Paul MacSwiney, told the crowd:

> The people of Ireland meet today to honour the man whose matchless genius won Emancipation, and whose fearless hand struck off the fetters whereby six millions of his countrymen were held in bondage in their own land....

It is of course a great irony that O'Connell's monument should contain the bullet holes of Easter week 1916 as it does, with O'Connell a constitutional nationalist who was opposed to the use of violence to bring about political ends. This statue quite literally saw Irish nationalism move from a constitutional movement to an insurrectionist one, when it found itself caught between the sniper fire of Sackville Street and the rooftops of Trinity College Dublin. One wonders what O'Connell would have thought of James Connolly, one of the leaders of that rebellion, giving the title 'A Chapter of Horrors: Daniel O'Connell and the Working Class' to a chapter in his excellent *Labour in Irish History*!

Yet it is so often forgotten today that while Irish republicans put bullet holes into this great statue, Irish loyalists almost done away with it. On 27 December 1969, an explosion at 4.30 a.m. damaged the statue representing the 'Winged Victory of Courage'. This attack was later claimed by the Ulster Volunteer Force.

The figure of Courage in the statue ironically contains a bullet hole of Easter 1916 itself. She is shown strangling a serpent, with her left hand resting on a fasces. In the breast of this figure perhaps the bullet hole with which the most Dubliners are familiar is found.

The explosion rocked the capital, with one taxi driver telling the *Irish Press* that 'the whole car and the bridge seemed to shake with the explosion. It was one tremendous wallop and then the crash of glass almost together.'

Incredibly, in the days following the bombing of the monument, an explosion occurred at Ship Street near Dublin Castle and the Detective Unit of the Gardai. It was stressed in media reports that it was believed

A vintage postcard image of the O'Connell monument.
(Fallon Collection)

no connection existed between these explosions, yet reports into this explosion in the *Irish Independent* noted that:

A phone call received at Independent House on Saturday night named three of the five Belfast men who, the callers said, were responsible for the monument explosion. The anonymous caller said the men were all members of an illegal organisation and that two of them were explosives experts and ex-army sergeants who had been discharged three months ago from the Royal Rangers for suspected political activity.

The bombing of the O'Connell monument was not the first attack on an Irish nationalist monument in the south by Ulster Loyalists, nor was it to be the last. Wolfe Tone's grave at Bodenstown had been attacked too – the irony of Northern Protestants attacking the graveside of a leading United Irishman was lost on many at the time. Later, in 1971, an explosion would destroy the Wolfe Tone statue at Saint Stephen's Green. Newspaper reports noted that 'the statue was wrecked, leaving only the base. Huge slabs of the bronze sculpture were hurled 20 feet in the air.'

The attacks on O'Connell and Tone are interesting as much has been written on statues from the other political tradition that were attacked and destroyed in Dublin, but little is said of the attacks on Irish nationalist icons. It is undeniable that attacks on monuments like the King William of Orange statue on College Green, Nelson's Pillar, Lord Gough's monument in the Phoenix Park and others represented a dangerous sort of cultural warfare, but it should be remembered that loyalists too engaged in such attacks. Dublin is fortunate that many lives were not lost while this dangerous game was being played over the iconography of the Irish capital.

30.

Early Days of stand-up comedy in Dublin

Today, stand-up comedy is a multi-million Euro business. Comics like Dara O'Briain and Tommy Tiernan regularly do stints of ten or more nights in Vicar Street, Michael McIntyre can sell out the O2 twice over, dozens of comedians release DVDs for the Christmas market and a whole range of venues like the Laughter Lounge on Eden Quay, the Comedy Cellar at the International, Stand Up at Bankers pub and the Ha'Penny Bridge Inn offer people comedy seven nights a week.

This wasn't always the case.

From the late 1970s to the late 1980s, comics struggled to establish comedy nights in the upstairs of pubs, backrooms of hotels and theatres in the city. The history of stand-up comedy in Ireland is quite an overlooked subject, and besides Deirde Falvey and Stephon Dixon's fantastic *Gift of the Gag: The Explosion in Irish Comedy* (1999), nothing has really been written on the topic.

Particularly interesting and forgotten is the development of Irish stand-up from the birth of 'alternative comedy' in the mid 1970s to the establishment of the the Comedy Cellar in the International Bar on Wicklow Street in 1988. The groundwork that a small number of people did in these early years helped to nurture and develop the scene into what it now is today.

It is believed that Dublin's first ever stand-up comedy club was started in the 29 Club in the basement of The Holyrood Hotel on Harcourt Street in the mid 1970s by a Scottish performance artist called Oscar McLellan.

The 1970s were, in many ways, dark times for comedy in this country. The first so-called 'Festival of Humour' took place in May 1978 in Virginia, Co. Cavan. Things can be summed up by the fact that the chairman of the festival committee was the local priest Father Pat Morris. These were the days of Hal Roach at the Jury's Irish Cabaret and Jimmy O'Dea.

Unlike the current brand of 'king of blarney' Irish comedy, a new generation of jokers were beginning to assert themselves, particularly in the Dram Socs and Rag Weeks of the island's colleges. In UCD, Billy McGrath/ Magra, Paddy Murray and Brendan Martin formed a sketch group called 'the Spike Milligan Comedy Machine' known simply as 'The Machine'. Dermot Morgan (of *Father Ted* fame) wasn't too far behind, and later performed as 'Big Gom and the Imbeciles' with Billy in Theatre L.

Spurred on by the explosion, perhaps even a revolution, of intelligent, often anarchic, progressive stand-up (described in a phrase coined by Tony Allen as 'Alternative Comedy') in London's Comedy Store by comics such as Alexi Sayle, Andy de la Tour and Pauline Melville, and in *The Comic Strip*, which soon followed, by comics such as Rik Mayall, Ade Edmondson, Nigel Planer and French and Saunders, stand-up comics in Dublin began testing the water and starting up their own nights.

From the late 1970s and throughout the 1980s in venues like the Hollyrood Hotel on Harcourt Street, the Project Arts Centre on East Essex Street, McGonagles on South Anne Street, the Mansion House on Dawson Street and the Sportman's Inn (now Kiely's) in Mount Merrion, up-and-coming actors, comics and messers like Billy McGrath/Magra, Mannix Flynn, Paul Malone, Michael Redmond, Roisin Sheeran, Ian McPherson, Helen Morrissey, Kevin McAleer, Owen Roe (a.k.a. Ronald Raygun) and Gerry Lavelle took to the stage and tested the boundaries. Sharing the same venues and many of the same values, this exciting new brand of 'alternative comedy' ruffled the feathers of the established comedy scene as much as Punk did to music.

In 1984, the Comedy Store (Dublin) ambitiously released its own live L.P. The 13-track L.P. was recorded live at the Project Arts Centre by Eerie Music Mobile, engineered by Johnny Byrne and Peter Eades, mixed and edited by Slimmer Twins and produced by Stand Treasual (a.k.a. Billy McGrath). The executive producer was MCD's Dennis Desmond.

Slowly but surely, modern 'alternative' stand-up comedy began to assert itself, influence a whole new generation and gain credibility. By the late 1980s, this opened up the path for 'Mr Trellis' (Ardal O'Hanlon, Barry Murphy and Kevin Gildea) and the 'Quack Squad' (Joe Rooney and Paul Tylak) to open up the Comedy Cellar in the International Bar.

Thus starting the next chapter of Dublin's standup history....

31.

'A Lunatic Fringe Element' at Richmond Park

While Dalymount Park is associated with some incredible concerts, including an appearance by Bob Marley, it was a League of Ireland ground on the southside of the capital that hosted what was supposedly Ireland's first ever outdoor rock festival. On 4 September 1970, Richmond Park played host to an outdoor festival involving both local and international acts. The event was headlined by Mungo Jerry, but also included a performance from Dubliners Thin Lizzy.

Newspaper reports from the time suggest that there was a real fear of what kind of element would be attracted to outdoor music festivals in the capital.

In the build-up to the event, the *Irish Press* wrote of fears that a 'lunatic fringe element' would be drawn to an outdoor rock concert. The *Irish Independent* reported that something in the region of 4,000 people had been expected to attend the festival, and that the ground could potentially hold double that. Repeating the sort of tone of the *Irish Press* piece, the paper wrote that 'fears of rowdyism' existed prior to the event, but that these were dispelled by officials at Saint Patrick's Athletic.

In the end, the festival proved to be an absolute disaster. 'I've been to better wakes' was a quote from one discontented young punter in *The Irish Times*, which ran with the headline 'Open Air Festival Hardly Pops'. The paper noted that only several hundred young people had attended the festival, perhaps unsurprising giving the scare tactics in the media in the run-up to the event.

Mungo Jerry headlined the show, yet *The Irish Times* did not have much to say of their appearance, noting only that 'they appeared finally, like post-Christmas tinsel, on a shabby stand.'

Of course, while Thin Lizzy are viewed as a legendary Dublin band today, at the time they were a new prospect. They had only formed in late 1969, and released their first single two months prior to the Richmond Park performance.

32.

Lady Justice, Dublin Castle

Erected by the British authorities in 1751, our Lady Justice, or 'Iustitia', to credit her with her official title, has since kept a watchful eye on the tribunals and other proceedings in Dublin Castle's Inner Courtyard. Sitting atop the gate nearest City Hall, she betrays many of the characteristics of representations of her sort. Iustitia, in representing Justice, is generally to be portrayed as blindfolded; objective and blind to discrimination. Her scales are always to be in working order and perfectly level; support and opposition, innocent until proven guilty. Her double-edged sword, depicting reason and justice, should generally point downward, in a non-provocative manner.

Dublin's Iustitia, though, is unusual in several respects. Her eyes are unbound. There is an argument for this, for while the general precedent shows her eyes bound, there are other examples, such as the Old Bailey in London, in which her sight is unhindered. The scales she holds are far from level. Despite drilling holes in the bottom of the scales to let rainwater run out, which had been causing them to lean to one side or the other, they still lean towards the side of the gate where Revenue and the tax office is located. How typical. Her sword, again as with the Old Bailey, points upright, and Iustitia gazes at it with a satisfied grin on her face.

What really got to the people of Dublin when she was erected, however, is the direction in which she is facing. You will find depictions of Lady Justice on courthouses all over the world, and you will invariably find her looking out over the city. Only in Dublin does she face into the courtyard, turning her back on the people of the city. Dubliners, never slow out of the boxes, came up with the following epithet shortly after she was erected: 'There she stands, upon her station, with her face to the ground and her arse to the nation.'

33.

The mysterious case of Karl Schumann (a.k.a. Ashley Shoeman)

In September and October 1939, a 21-year-old 'coloured alien' by the name of Karl Schumann, who also used the alias Ashley Shoeman, was found sleeping, on at least two occasions, on the roof of the Polo Pavilion in the Phoenix Park.

It was heard in court that Schumann first arrived into Ireland, via Limerick, on a German steamer boat and decided that he 'did not want to go further'. Due to the fact that he reached Ireland in a German vessel, there was some confusion over his nationality.

He was described first in court in by Senior District Justice Little as a 'German from Cape Town'. However, Mr Donovan from the Chief Solicitor's Office raised the point that it 'was mere chance that he was on a German ship', and because of his South African birth he should be described as a 'British subject'. At the time, Schumann was living at an address in James's Street, but the house number was not given.

Schumann was again up in court in October 1939 for the same offence and here he was described as 'British national … born in Cape Town'. The case was dismissed by the judge.

That's when his trail ends.

I wonder what happened to Karl Schumann? Did he stay in Dublin? Return to his birthplace of Cape Town? Or perhaps make a new life in Britain?

No one seems to know.

34.

Gordon Banks, World Cup winner and supersaint

Some remarkable players have begun their careers in the League of Ireland before making the leap to UK football, but in the past a few famous British footballers wound down their careers with Irish sides, including a World Cup winner or two. Gordon Banks, the celebrated English goalkeeper who guarded the English net in their year of victory in 1966, once stood in goal for Saint Patrick's Athletic in Inchicore. Incredibly, by the time Banks played for the Saints, he had lost his vision in one eye following a car crash!

Banks played one game for the Saints: a home match against Dublin rivals Shamrock Rovers. Barry Bridges was managing the Saints at the time as playermanager. During the previous year, in 1976, Pat's had gained some attention by picking up Neil Martin, a former Hibernian F.C., Sunderland and Nottingham Forest striker, among other clubs. In fact, English player-manager Bridges had an impressive record himself, including but not limited to spells at Chelsea, Milwall and QPR.

The Irish Times of 1 October 1977 noted that Barry Bridges stated there was a 'fifty-fifty' chance that Banks would line out the next night in Richmond Park. Picked up from Fort Lauderdale in the United States, it all depended on clearance from the American F.A. The paper noted that 'the signing, which is likely to extract a sharp response from St Patrick's first choice goalkeeper, Mick O' Brien, represents the Dubliners' most enterprising move since Neil Martin joined the club last season'.

While it was common enough at the time for English players to semi-retire in the U.S. game, Banks signing to Pat's was a surprise to many. In the end, he was given clearance to perform and maintained a clean sheet, in a one-nil home victory over Rovers. He would never grace the pitch at Richmond Park again, and returned to the United States, seemingly unimpressed.

Barry Bridges remained at Pat's until February 1978, moving on to become player-manager of Sligo Rovers. Banks is only one former English international to briefly play in the Irish league. Geoff Hurst, Terry Venables (another Saint), Carlton Palmer and Bobby Charlton are just a small selection of others who have done the same. Banks can boast a 100% clean record sheet in Inchicore!

35.

The curious case of Robert C. and the bombing of the Spanish Cultural Institute

In March 1974, the recently opened Spanish Cultural Institute on Northumberland Road was petrol-bombed by suspected insurrectionary anarchists. It took three sections of the Dublin Fire Brigade to put out the fire, which badly charred the hall door.

The wife of the director of the Institute and her 10-month-old son were in the house at the time of the blast. Both escaped injury.

Passers-by told the Gardaí that they had seen two men running down the steps and getting into a blue Hillman Minx car parked a short distance from the house, shortly after the attack. The men were aged between 20 and 30, 5 ft. 9 ins., slim, with dark, shoulder-length hair and dark suits.

Soon after the attack, a man with an Irish accent telephoned the *Sunday Press* and said: 'I am speaking for the First of May group. We have exploded a bomb at the Spanish Cultural Institute. It is in retaliation for the murder today in Spain of the Spanish anarchist'. The anarchist in question was Salvador Puig Antich (26), a student, who was executed in Barcelona for killing a policeman in September 1973. Also executed that day was Polish citizen Heinz Ces, for shooting a Guardia Civil police officer in Tarragona.

On 8 March 1974, a letter was published in *The Irish Times* deploring the attack, and was signed by more than sixty UCD students and teachers. It stated that 'the Institute ... is exclusively concerned with cultural activities, and thousands of people have already availed themselves of its services, and know that these are offered without any political strings.' 'We hold no brief whatever for the Franco regime, political representation or any form of capital punishment', it added, and we 'deplore the execution of Spanish anarchists as much as any petrol-bomber thinks he does.'

In July 1974, a 24-year-old clerk called Robert C. (surname withheld for privacy), with an address on the South Circular Road, was sentenced to jail for seven years after admitting making a letter-bomb and leaving it outside the Iberian Airlines office on Grafton Street. He was also charged with armed robbery, and possession of firearms, ammunition and explosive substances. Three other individuals in their early 20s were also sentenced, the first for 'conspiring with others to cause explosions' and the other two for holding money that they knew had been stolen.

In January 1972, Robert C. was one of nine people up in court in connection with squatting in Frascati

House in Blackrock. The charges included 'making or having explosives' and assaulting a Garda by the name of John Munnely. Frascati House was threatened with demolition, and it would appear that these nine individuals who squatted were involved with the Dun Laoghaire Housing Action Group.

Among other items found in the possession of Robert C. during searches of his house in July 1974 was a notebook containing information on the Spanish Embassy in Dublin, the registration number of the Ambassador's car and the names of the Director of the Spanish Cultural Institute as well as those of his wife and son. One could come to the conclusion that Robert C. may have been involved in the attack on the Spanish Cultural Centre a few months before.

On 23 February 1975, Robert C. joined a hunger-strike with nine other prisoners in the Curragh Camp in protest against visiting conditions and the standard of food, as well as other grievances. By the 3 March, Robert was one of only four prisoners still on hunger-strike. The Prisoners' Rights Organisation picketed the Department of Justice and the Curragh Detention Centre in protest against the 'deplorable conditions' that had forced the non-political prisoners to start the strike. On 5 March, the hunger-strike came to an end. No details were available as to the condition of the prisoners or as to the reason why the strike was called off.

After his release, Robert presumably led a quiet, non-political life.

36.

The famous Vonolel, Dublin's war horse

One of the most unusual graves in Dublin is found at the Royal Hospital Kilmainham, and marks the final resting place of Vonolel, a bemedalled military horse and loyal companion of Field Marshall Earl Roberts, who saw action in Afghanistan and India in service to his master.

Vonolel was an Arab charger who had been purchased from a horse dealer in Bombay in March 1877 at the age of only four years old, and who would become the charger of the celebrated Earl Roberts during the Afghan Campaign of 1878–80. He had been present in the march from Kabul to Kandahar, and the *Navy and Army Illustrated* said in 1898 that he had 'acquitted himself with honour' on this trek, and had he been a human would undoubtedly have been mentioned in dispatches. Vonolel had been named after a famous Lushai chief, and for his heroics in the Afghan Campaign, *The Irish Times* of 21 October 1899 noted, was awarded the Kabul medal, with four clasps, and the bronze Kandahar Star. Vonolel had marched in the

Queen's Jubilee procession the year before, wearing his medals upon him, and the *Navy and Army Illustrated* reported a woman as being heard to ask if Earl Roberts had so many decorations that he was obliged to make his horse carry some!

Contemporary newspaper reports described Vonolel as 'a type of the highest class of Arab charger', and it was noted that 'he traces his descent from the best blood of the desert'.

From October 1895, Roberts assumed the post of Commander-in-Chief of British forces in Ireland, and Vonolel was retired to the Curragh in Kildare. Roberts would have been based at the Royal Hospital Kilmainham, and Vonolel's grave notes that he passed away while at the Royal Hospital in June 1899. News of Vonolel's death was carried by media all over the world, and the *Star* in New Zealand noted the deep sense of friendship that existed between Roberts and Vonolel, noting that they were said to be 'inseparable during the Field Marshall's brilliant career in India.'

Roberts was said to be heartbroken, and Vonolel was buried in the rose gardens of the hospital with full military honours. Upon Vonolel's grave his military exploits are acknowledged, as is his character. The headstone includes a poem, which reads:

There are men both good and wise
Who hold that in a future state
Dumb creatures we have cherished here below

Shall give us joyous greeting when
We pass the golden gate
Is it folly that I hope it may be so?

Vonolel was 29 years old at the time of his passing, and Earl Roberts would go on to see military action again in the Second Boer War. When he died in 1914, Roberts was buried in Saint Paul's Cathedral. An equestrian statue of Roberts is found on Horse Guards Parade in London.

37.

Stompin' George and The Magnet

Stompin' George' Verschoyle (62) from Artane in North Dublin has been a dominant figure in the Irish rockabilly scene for over four decades. For the first time ever, he has agreed to be interviewed about his life, and the Dublin rock 'n' roll scene of the 1970s and 1980s in which he played such a pivotal role.

George was born into a musical family. His mother was a graduate of the National School of Music, and George and his younger sister were sent to piano lessons when they were younger, but he soon got bored. 'The teacher was into light classical; I wanted to be the next Jerry Lee Lewis', he recalls.

At the age of nine, George began listening to Jimmy Savile's *The Teen and Twenty Disc Club* and *Jack Jackson's Jukebox Show* on Radio Luxembourg. Though he usually was put to bed at around 8 p.m., he convinced his mother to wake him up at 10.55 p.m. on Sundays so he could listen to Barry Aldis' *Top Twenty* till midnight. In the early 1960s, the BBC presented a radio documentary on the history of rock

141

'n' roll, which George taped on a reel-to-reel (he still has the tapes). George pinpoints this series and its opening track, 'Tongue Tied Jill' by Charlie Feathers, as introducing him to what was to become an essential part of his life: rockabilly.

Every Saturday night, George and a mixed group of around 20 friends would go down to the local hop in Chanel College in Coolock. One night the DJs (Don and Gerry) failed to turn up and so George, at the age of 14, offered to step in. This was his first stint at DJing. The year was 1962. After that first night, George began standing in for Don and Gerry on a regular basis.

After gaining experience and confidence, he was offered the role of resident DJ in The Flamingo Club on O'Connell Street, which opened in September 1966. He stayed there for two years, playing a mix of 1950s rock 'n' roll and 60s sounds.

George took a break from spinning records for a couple of years until he bumped into a fellow rockabilly fan called 'Rockin' Kevin' in his local, The Bachelor Inn. The pair hit it off, and they soon began organising 'record hops' in the upstairs function room.

The nights were a success, and they soon outgrew The Bachelor and moved to The Regent Hotel on D'Olier Street. It was at this time that several of the local biker groups began attending the nights, including the Road Rockers and the Viking chapter of the Hells Angels as well as other bikers. Unlike most media stereotypes, the Dublin bikers were a friendly bunch, and not the stereotypical violent type normally portrayed.

A fire that destroyed the hotel a couple of years later meant the venue had to change and The Mondello Club was suggested by biker Tony Kelly. George used to organise a bus from The Bachelor pub to The Mondello and back every Sunday.

Around 1977, they moved again; this time to Goulding's Social Club on Townsend Street. A year later, George joined Capitol Radio, which was based a few doors down from The Bachelor, where he presented a show playing the 'best in rock 'n' roll and rockabilly'. He remembers that a lot of listeners 'used to phone and write in asking why there weren't any rockabilly hops in town.'

At the time, the only places you could find rockabilly was Sunday nights in Toners where Rocky De Valera & The Grave Diggers played Dr Feelgoodinspired rock 'n' roll, or Friday nights in The Magnet Bar on Pearse Street, where Hurricane Johnny & The Jets played rock 'n' roll covers.

George went to see The Jets in The Magnet a couple of times, and decided that the venue would be perfect for a record hop. He spoke to Liam Lynch, The Magnet's owner, about taking over Monday nights and the rest, as they say, 'is history'.

The Magnet on Monday nights, which started in September 1978 and ended in March 1983, has since gone down in Dublin rock 'n' roll history, with many regarding it as the glory days of the Irish rockabilly revival scene.

It 'was an old type workingman's pub', whose upstairs venue could hold 200 people. George explains that the night attracted a 'mix of people including bikers, teds, mods, rockers and the odd punk'. In their four and a half years there, there was never any major trouble. He explains this was because people 'policed themselves' because they didn't want to risk losing the venue as there was 'nowhere else to go for a good night's music'.

The 1980s saw a huge rockabilly revival in the UK, with young bands like The Sunsets, Crazy Cavan and The Rhythm Rockers, The Polecats, The Shakin' Pyramids and the American-born band The Stray Cats breaking the charts. Unlike some other original rockabilly fans, who viewed this new generation of rockers as 'too punchy' or 'too commercial', George thought for the most part 'they were helping to bring the music to a much wider audience'. He makes it clear, however, that he 'didn't like or agree with the likes of Showaddywaddy or Mud, who did nothing for rockabilly.'

The two visits of the Scottish group The Shakin' Pyramids were definitely the 'high point of our years in The Magnet', George says. 'I know of people there on the night and who still reckon it was one of the best gigs seen in Dublin. I have seen many bands and artists over the years, including The Beatles, but I was never at a gig like the Pyramids, it was electric.'

When The Magnet closed, George felt that their rock 'n' roll nights 'had more or less run their course already and it was the right time to leave'. Most felt it was time to take a break anyway. 'A lot of the regulars had moved on with their lives, got married, went abroad to work' or had 'taken up golf'. George got married to Fran in 1981, and his first daughter was born in September 1981. It was time to take a break from music.

It didn't last long, however, and in the mid 1980s, George teamed up with another friend 'Boppin' Billy' and started a residency in The Underground in Dame street, which ran for 18 months. After that, they had a several month stint in The St Laurence Hotel in Howth followed by a pub on Camden Street and finally a little wine bar/restaurant called Blazes on Essex Street.

By this stage, George and his crew were making a name for themselves in the city. They were invited to play at a 30th birthday for the Guinness family in Leixlip, and six wrap-up gigs for various film shoots. At one of the 'wraps' held in a stately house outside Bray, when the place was rockin' at 5 a.m. and no one wanted to go home, George recalls that 'a famous RTÉ DJ of the time came over to us and said he had never in all his years heard such amazing music – this sort of sums up what rockabilly music is!'

Their final gig together was in The Hard Rock Café, but 'it was doomed from the start as they would only give us Sunday nights starting at 11 p.m.' They did manage, however, to get an invite to support The Pogues at the National Stadium. 'That was really interesting as there were about 2,000 people at the gig and they would break out into spontaneous applause after a piece of rare rockabilly'. George reckons it was 'possibly the first time most of them had ever heard of Charlie Feathers or Herbie Duncan!'

Stompin' George is still DJing and boppin' after 48 years. He should be an inspiration to us all.

38.

Grangegorman Military Cemetery

Grangegorman Military Cemetery lies a mere two and a half miles from the GPO, but ask any Dubliner about its existence or who's buried there and you will be met with a blank face from the vast majority. Located on Blackhorse Avenue, not far from The Hole in the Wall pub, it is the resting place of British soldiers who died or were killed in action on this island. Whereas these days the bodies of British soldiers killed in action are brought home and buried with full military honours, this was not always the case. To save expense, the British Empire had a rule of burying her soldiers where they died.

Whilst the interest for Irish people visiting the Cemetery is likely to be focussed towards those who died in the Easter Rising and the War of Independence, there are also graves scattered around of ex-soldiers who came, or in many cases were sent, here to recover from wounds received in the trenches of the First World War. There is also a long line of graves for those who died in the sinking of the RMS Leinster in 1918.

The number of military casualties, not counting military police, in the Easter Rebellion is estimated to be around the 140 mark. Those killed served a variety of different battalions, though most notably, large numbers came from the South Staffordshire Regiment; a Regiment subsequently accused of bayoneting 15 innocent civilians to death on North King Street towards the end of the week, and the Sherwood Foresters, killed in the Battle for Mount Street Bridge.

Battalion badges are marked on each of the headstones, along with the name of the soldier buried there, their rank and the date of their death, whilst a small few have personal inscriptions. Matching the battalions and dates from the gravestones with the known events in Easter week can give us an idea of where these British soldiers met their deaths. A grave bearing the date 25 April and the soldier's battalion, the 5th Lancers, would suggest, for example, that he was wounded at the ambush of the ammunitions convoy by Ned Daly's Four Courts Garrison and died the following day.

Unlike the rebel dead, not many names stand out. One headstone that does, though, is that of Guy Vickery Pinfield. Pinfield, like a majority of the soldiers (and indeed rebels) involved in Easter Week, was a young man, only 21 years of age. Attached to the 8th King's Royal Irish Hussars, he was shot through the heart whilst on guard duty at Dublin Castle on 24 April and was buried in a temporary grave in a garden in the Castle, where he lay for 46 years until he was exhumed and reburied in his current plot in Grangegorman. His name came to light in 2011 when he came up in several Irish media outlets when a locket dedicated to his memory sold at an auction in England for £800, twice its original estimate. A plaque dedicated to his memory can be found in Saint Patrick's Cathedral.

The cemetery is also home to the final resting place of Algernon Lucas and Basil Henry Worsley Worswick, both shot by their own side (alongside two civilians) in the Guinness Brewery, falsely accused of aiding the rebels in what is one of the strangest stories from Easter Week. The death of Lucas, alongside Guinness employee William John Rice, was ordered by Company Quartermaster Sergeant Robert Flood of the 5th Battalion Royal Dublin Fusiliers, who later stood trial for the murders, but was acquitted. In his defence during his Court Martial he said that he believed the men to have been acting suspiciously; he believed them to be Sinn Féin spies and had them executed rather than imprisoned for fear of weakening his garrison. No enquiry took place in relation to the death of Worsley Worswick or the Guinness employee known as Dockeray who was shot alongside him.

The graveyard is maintained to Commonwealth War Graves Commission standards, and as such is impeccable. It is easy to forget that there were two sides of the story on Easter Week; alongside the rebel dead lay the bodies of English soldiers, many of whom were members of the army as a result of, as Connolly called it, 'conscription by starvation.' Many had not fired a rifle in anger before, and found themselves being shot down leading repeated charges on Mount Street Bridge under the orders of contemptuous senior offices. Only hours previously many had believed they were destined for France.

39.

Stein Opticians

The Irish-Jewish family Stein have run an optician's in Dublin for nearly seventy years. They are perhaps best known for their 1983 'David vs Goliath' battle, where they fought bitterly to save their practice on Harcourt Road from the developer's bulldozer.

Dublin born Mendel Stein (1915–2000) grew up in Victoria Street in the heart of Portobello, then known as 'Little Jerusalem'. Studying to become an ophthalmic optician, he set up his practice at 36 Harcourt Road in 1944.

For the next 41 years, he remained one of the most popular opticians in the city, and his practice, known as 'The Eye', became 'a place for encounter, conversation and spirited views on the life of Harcourt Road and the universe beyond'. Mendel became close friends with Micheál MacLiammóir, Hilton Edwards, Harry Kernoff and others at the heart of Dublin's art and theatre scenes.

Everything was going well until 1983, when the Clancourt Group announced that they wanted to build a seven-storey office block, which meant demolishing the terrace to make way for the new Harcourt Centre.

Stein's Opticians, Grantham St. (Paul Reynolds)

While other property owners and lessees of buildings due for demolition accepted the substantial compensation, Mendel decided that he wasn't going to give in so easily. He said that he would not leave until they gave him a new shop in the immediate vicinity and a guarantee that his (beautiful) shopfront would be preserved.

This window of the shopfront was 'in the shape of an eye, whose pupil is reflected in a circular mirror on a facing wall inside'. Frank McDonald of *The Irish Times* described it at the time as 'a masterpiece of its period

[that] arguably should have been officially listed for preservation'.

By the end of it, his single-storey shop was the only surviving remnant of Harcourt Road, despite the fact that the tiny building was perched on the edge of a 'cliff' while the new block was under construction. The late Brendan Glacken later recalled a story that during this time a young, quick-witted Dubliner shouted in to Mendel: 'Hey, mister, your extension is coming on great!'

Spurred on by local support, Mendel held out and eventually received a guarantee that the shop would be taken down intact and re-erected at a new location in nearby Grantham Street off Camden Street.

Joined at this stage in the practice by his daughter Ameila, Mendel worked at his new Grantham Street address until he reached his 80s. He passed away in June 2000.

Amelia, an award-winning photographer who has worked with Irish artists such as The Hothouse Flowers, Aslan and The Cranberries, ran the family optician business from 4 Camden Market, Grantham Street until its closure in 213.

40.

Raising the red flag over the Rotunda, 1922

The seizure of the Rotunda concert hall by a reasonably large group of unemployed workers, and the hoisting of the red flag over the premises, remains one of the more bizarre events of the Irish revolutionary period.

In his excellent history of the ITGWU, *The Irish Transport and General Workers' Union: The Formative Years*, C. Desmond Greaves wrote that, early in 1922, 'industrial conflict took the form of individual struggles rather than a concerted class war.' The occupation of the Rotunda came two days after the foundation of the new state, and was perhaps the earliest example of class anger within it, a direct response to the existing high levels of unemployment.

One of the leading figures of this occupation was Liam O' Flaherty, today well known as the author of *The Informer*, the classic novel, but then acting as a dedicated socialist.

He, like so many other unemployed men in Dublin, had served in the Great War, serving with the Irish Guards. He had been on a strange journey before returning to Dublin. After being invalided out of the British forces, O'Flaherty found himself involved in radical politics in Canada and the United States. For a period he was involved with the Industrial Workers' of the World trade union, and later the Communist Party of the USA. He arrived back in Ireland at Christmas 1921, with new political ideas.

On 18 January 1922, a group of unemployed Dublin workers seized the concert hall of the Rotunda. *The Irish Times* of the following day noted that: 'The unemployed in Dublin have seized the concert room at the Rotunda, and they declare that they will hold that part of the building until they are removed, as a protest against the apathy of the authorities.' The paper said that 'from one of the windows the red flag flies.'

Liam O' Flaherty, as chairman of the 'Council of Unemployed', spoke to the paper about the refusal of the men to leave the premises, stating that no physical resistance would be put up against the police and that the protest was a peaceful one, yet they intended to stay where they were. 'If we were taken to court, we would not recognise the court, because the Government that does not redress our grievances is not worth recognising', O' Flaherty told journalists.

A manifesto was issued by the occupiers, the first publication of O' Flaherty. Two days into the occupation, around 200 men were present.

It was noted by *The Irish Times* that a maintenance fund had been established, with Boland's Bakery on

Capel Street making a grant of 500 loaves to the men. The paper also noted that sporadic concerts had taken place inside the occupation, and that the men had 'paraded Parnell Square.'

Of course, many Dubliners were extremely hostile to the sight of the red flag in Dublin. Angry demonstrations occurred each night during the occupation, and the *Irish Independent* noted (21 January) that:

About 8.30 last night a hostile crowd of about 500 assembled in Cavendish Row, and indulged in shouts and derisive cheers. About 10 p.m. a young fellow made an attempt to reach the red flag hung out from a window, but fell to the ground. He was taken to Jervis St. Hospital, but he was not detained.

When the flag was removed, the crowd cheered loudly. It was only thanks to the Dublin Metropolitan Police and the 'Republican Police' that those inside the Rotunda were unharmed as the crowd stormed the building. It was becoming clear that the occupation was not sustainable. On the Thursday night, a member of the occupying group had been attacked collecting money near the premises, and since then tensions had been high.

The occupation, which had begun on Wednesday, was to end late on Saturday night. As the aggression outside intensified, shots were fired over the heads of the mob from inside the hall. Just before midnight, and under the protection of the police, the occupiers left the building and the crowd departed without incident. O' Flaherty quickly took off for Cork, though he would later see action in the capital once more when he took part in the Civil War.

41.

Looking back at The Blades

Socially conscious, musically gifted and uncompromising in their attitude towards the manipulative music industry, The Blades remain one the most revered and important Irish bands of all time.

The genius of Paul Cleary, lead singer and songwriter of the band, lay in his ability to craft both memorable love songs and standout tracks about the critical issues of his generation: boredom, unemployment and a crippling recession. Class-conscious and sympathetic to socialist politics, Cleary 'tried to get that into (his) music without browbeating people'.

Lending support to various worthwhile causes, The Blades played numerous benefit gigs throughout the 1980s. These included gigs for Rock Against Sexism in UCD in February 1980, for the families of those who died in the Stardust fire in 1981, for the pro-choice Anti-Amendment campaign in September 1982 and for the Dunnes Stores anti-apartheid striking workers in January 1985. In 1986, they famously shunned the 'back-slapping' Self-Aid to play the left-wing Rock The System one-day music festival at Liberty Hall.

The Blades' roots lay in their working-class, southeast Dublin 4 neighbourhood of Ringsend. Spurred into action by the Punk explosion, they made their live debut as a five-piece at their local Catholic Young Men's Society (CYMS) Hall in the summer of 1977. Ironically, the plug was pulled on the gig early when the sound engineer took exception to the band playing God Save the Queen; not understanding it was The Sex Pistols' version!

Subsequently, with Cleary on bass, his brother Lar on guitar and childhood friend Pat Larkin on drums, the band were a formidable trio. The sharply dressed, melodic post-Punk outfit played 'short, punchy, guitardriven songs' that suited the live, intense atmosphere of their first home, The Magnet, a tough local bar on Pearse Street. These early gigs, only enjoyed by a room full of 40 or so Mods and Soul Boys, went down as some of the best in Dublin's live music history.

A year later, they were in The Baggot Inn playing a now famous six-week residency with another fledging Dublin band: U2. Dave Fanning, who DJed, recalls that parts of the crowd would leave straight after The Blades, ignoring U2. The two bands couldn't have been more different. While Cleary and co. would unleash an assault of high-tempo, three-minute pop/soul numbers, Bono used to come on stage and tell the 'crowd of a dream he had the night before'.

This first line up of The Blades, which lasted from 1977 to 1982, released two fantastic singles; the catchy summer pop classic 'Hot For You' in 1980, followed a year later with the more mature 'Ghost of a Chance', which dealt with love across the class divide. Disenchanted with the failure of Energy Records to proceed with the planned LP, Lar and Pat left the band.

Replaced by bassist Brian Foley (ex. The Vipers) and drummer Jake Reilly, Cleary moved and took over guitar duties. Coupled with the horns section of the Blues Brass, a 'couple of renegade musicians from The Artane Boys Band', this more developed and ambitious model recorded an LP with Elektra, but in a nasty turn of events the record company, who had recently lost a substantial amount trying to break Howard Jones into the American market, decided not to release it.

Left with a finished product (recorded in London with The Smiths' producer John Porter) but with little else, The Blades found themselves in a frustrating scenario. Luckily, the record was eventually released, to critical acclaim, by the pioneering Irish label Reekus. Cleary, a lifelong fan of George Orwell, titled the LP *The Last Man In Europe,* the original choice of name for *Nineteen Eighty-Four*.

Before their one and only studio album was released, The Blades brought out three first-rate singles. The guitar-driven 'The Bride Wore White' in March 1982 was voted single of the year in the *Hot Press* National Poll, with Cleary also winning

Best Irish Songwriter, beating Bono, Van Morrison and Phil Lynott. It was followed later that year by 'Revelations Of Heartbreak', the multi-layered brass-tastic dancefloor stomper.

Then in 1983 The Blades released what is often regarded as their masterpiece: the seminal 'Downmarket'. In little under four minutes and two verses, Cleary managed to capture the mood of the whole country in the bleak 1980s recession using the specific personal experience of a young man waking up in an 'unfamiliar bedroom' after a one-night stand. His 'successful' encounter is contrasted against the 'problems of the nation'. Stuck in a city that is 'black and white and grey', the protagonist, both physically and metaphorically, has no way of finding short or long-term relief from Dublin (such as that an airport or station could offer), but instead finds himself waiting at a bus stop the next morning.

One more single ('Last Man In Europe') and a fantastic collection of their 1980–1985 recordings (*Raytown Revisited*) later, The Blades split up in 1986. Cleary subsequently formed The Partisans and today plays with well-respected pub-rock band The Cajun Kings.

The Blades are fondly remembered by those who were lucky enough to see them in action, and are constantly being discovered by a new generation of fans. They remain one of the best Irish bands of all time, and one of the few who attempted to address the social issues of their time.

Comments from Facebook:

Paul Jennings: 'I only seen them once. It was their second or third last gig but that was enough to say they were the finest Dublin/Irish band I've ever seen live ... Cleary was a genius.'

Seamus Duggan: 'Saw The Blades in an L-shaped room in O'Shea's hotel in Bray and still remember the difficulty of getting to the corner to actually see them. That, and the power of the brass. Also saw them in the National Stadium and there was a real sense that they were a communal band, who expressed what their audience was thinking. Paul's songs were always clever without being smart, if that makes sense. 'Downmarket' was almost an anthem, but not in the stadium rock sense. An anthem for all those who didn't put their fists in the air, for those who were suspicious of the easy answers, even their own.'

Des Flanagan: 'They were the first real band I'd ever seen live, The White Horse Hotel, Drogheda. I have to admit I had butterflies in my stomach before the gig cos I had no idea what was in store. I was completely blown away, my ears buzzed for days after it cos it was so loud, they really were top draw. My love for music went up another level that night. Fantastic singer, fantastic songwriter!!'

C Anthony Farrell: 'To see The Blades live brought you a high. The build up to gigs in the Baggot started the moment I finished in Barrow

Street, down the road from Paul's family home ... The songs he wrote about social issues were on par with Weller and Bragg.'

Ken Sweeney: 'At the time the Irish music scene was awash with U2 clones and bad New Romantics trying to ape Spandau Ballet. Myself and my friends didn't want to walk around the Ilac Centre (in Dublin) dressed as pirates. Here were three lads from Ringsend we could relate to, with suits and great pop songs. Paul Cleary was an immensely talented yet modest man. The singles just got better and better. Songs like 'Downmarket' reflected the Ireland we lived in. I can still remember how exciting it was when The Blades opened gigs with Paul hammering out the A chord intro to 'The Last Man In Europe'. But whoever let them put Paul Cleary's suit from Hairy Legs on Liffey Street on the sleeve of 'Raytown Revisited'? That was a mistake.'

David Harris: 'Seen The Blades a fair few times in the TV Club and the Baggot ... It started with putting on your best clobber, downing a flagon of merry down and the 48a into Charlemont Street and then the TV Club. Then Paul walking on stage with his white Fred Perry and beret and then it was a hundred miles an hour – 'Hot For You', 'Ghost Of A Chance', 'The Bride Wore White' – all classics. You were there with your best mates and life was great, we have a lot to thank The Blades for.'

Louise Duggan: 'The Mercantile, TV club, Galway, Drogheda. Trinity Ball, UCD and Fridays at the Baggot – wherever – I just was blown away how they captured the combination of emotional and social issues, they belted them out with attitude and a fantastic melody. We all gathered to be on the same team, singing out the songs like a ritual, watching the sweat pouring from Cleary, with the occasional smile. As time passed the brass came along and wow – the music, the words in the songs, the passion of the band ... just couldn't be beat.'

Proinsías Ó Baróid: 'The Blades looked cool in photo shoots, gave good interviews, sincere and modest, always underrating themselves (unlike many recognition vultures today and then) and toured like hell around the country. Ireland back then was arguably a few years behind England in trends and music related 'scenes', which hung on a bit longer over here. As a result there were still a lot of young people in Ireland into the Mod or Ska scene (some even just getting into it), which had left the mainstream in England really with the end of the Jam in '82, and The Specials. The Blades filled that void here for several years.

42.

Buck Whaley and the Hellfire Club

Dublin has had its fair share of hell-raisers in the past, which has contributed much to the folklore of the city. While many haven't heard of The Blasters, who were investigated by the old Irish Parliament in the 1730s for their rumoured Satanist behaviour, the Hellfire Club has entered the folk memory of the city.

The Hellfire Club was founded by the Duke of Wharton in London in 1719. Membership of the club was excessively exclusive and open only to rich, landed gentry. These rakes or wastrels of high society were known as 'Bucks', and their behaviour came to be viewed as an open affront to the church as their general activity revolved around drinking and blaspheming with gambling and wanton violence thrown in for good measure. Their motto was a warped nod to Rabelais' Theatre of the Absurd; '*Fais ce que tu voudras*,' or 'Do as thou wilt.' While Rabelais' statement is now generally agreed to mean that men born free are inherently moral, Wharton's club was as far from morality as you can get, and came to an end in 1721 when George I put forward a bill 'against 'horrid impieties'' aimed specifically at the Hellfire Club.

The Dublin Hellfire Club was founded shortly after the London club's demise by Colonel Jack St Leger, the son of a rich landowner from Kildare, and Richard Parsons, the First Earl of Rosse, who also happened to be the founder of the first Irish Lodge of Freemasons. The club had various meeting spots around Dublin, including Daly's Club, established on College Green in 1750, and The Eagle Tavern on Cork Hill, which was founded by Parsons sometime around 1735. Daly's was an opulent building, facing on to the old Parliament. In 1794, *The European* magazine and *London Review* referred to it, saying: 'The God of Cards and Dice has a Temple, called Daly's, dedicated to his honour in Dublin, much more magnificent than any Temple to be found in that City dedicated to the God of the Universe.' Daly's fell into decline when the rival Kildare Street Club poached many of its members after a fall-out in 1787. Their Eagle Tavern is no more, having been lost to the regeneration of Cork Hill through the centuries.

Meetings of the Hellfire Club routinely began with members sitting around a table, upon which was placed a large bowl containing a concoction dubbed 'scaltheen', a mixture of Irish whiskey and melted butter. The Bucks would toast the Devil and, after drinking to the damnation of the Church, folklore has it they would pour the remaining scaltheen over a cat and set fire to the poor creature.

While the club met in various places in the city, in the folklore of Dublin it has become synonymous with Montpellier Hill in the Dublin Mountains, not far from Rathfarnham. As David Ryan has detailed in his excellent study of the Hellfire Club, there is no solid evidence they ever did meet here, but there are compelling stories. We know that the structure was built as a hunting lodge around 1725 on land purchased by William Connolly, speaker in the Irish House of Commons, and Ireland's richest man at the time of his death. It was said that an ancient Cairn was demolished during the construction of the lodge, and that many of its stones were used in the construction of the lodge's slated roof. When a powerful storm damaged the roof, superstitious locals attributed it to the destruction of the Cairn.

In folklore, it has been told that the Bucks used the building as a headquarters for about 15 years, until they ruined it around 1740. One story has it that the burning of the Montpelier lodge can be attributed to Richard Chappell Whaley.

Richard Chappell Whaley's nickname was 'Burn-Chapel' Whaley because of his hatred of religion and his penchant for amusing himself on Sundays by riding around Dublin setting fire to the thatched roofs of Catholic chapels. At the age of 59, he married a woman 40 years his junior. Their son, Thomas 'Buck' Whaley was to become the most famous Buck of all.

Born in 1766, it was obvious from a young age that Buck Whaley had inherited his father's immoral streak. In his memoirs, he declared that he had taken it upon himself upon his father's death to 'defy God and man in [his] nightly revels'. Buck Whaley inherited a huge fortune after his father's death, and at the age of 16 was granted a yearly allowance of £900. His upbringing was spent between tutors in England and France before returning home to Dublin having spent some time in a Marseilles jail. Obviously having inherited his father's blasphemous, as well as immoral, streak, he was imprisoned, having 'insulted, violently assaulted and raised his sacrilegious hands against a Priest.' He escaped a long sentence after being secreted out of the country by a lawyer friend of the family.

While his inheritance at the time was huge, he won an even greater fortune from some bizarre wagers. Two of these wagers are infamous, and have been widely reported. The first, a wager with the Duke of Leinster, saw him riding to Jerusalem and back within a year. He accomplished this, and for his troubles made a profit of £7,000, the wager being for £15,000 and the trip costing £8,000. Far from a pious pilgrimage, he later boasted of playing handball against Jerusalem's holy walls. On another occasion, for a wager of £12,000, he rode a white Arab stallion from the drawing-room on the second floor of his father's house on Stephen's Green over a carriage parked outside the door and onto the street 25 feet below. He broke his leg in the fall, but unsurprisingly the horse was killed.

Mounting debts, and finally having come across something of a conscience, Buck Whaley moved with his wife to the Isle of Man, where he built a house on scattered Irish soil he imported, and there he wrote his memoirs. Repentant in his misery, he wrote 'I thought that a faithful picture of my youthful eccentricities, drawn with justice and impartiality, would not be unacceptable to my country-men, and particularly to my younger friends, who will find some few examples which they may follow with advantage, but many more which they ought to avoid.' He died in 1800 at the age of 34 from rheumatic fever whilst travelling from Liverpool to London. His death signalled the end for the Dublin Hellfire Club.

43·

Seán Treacy Street

Seán Treacy is a character of great importance to the War of Independence period; indeed he was among the men of the Third Tipperary Brigade who fired the opening shots of that conflict at the Soloheadbeg ambush. Treacy would lose his life on 14 October 1920 on the streets of Dublin, owing to a shoot-out on Talbot Street that would also leave Gilbert Price of the British Secret Service lying dead on the street. A small plaque on Talbot Street today marks the spot where Treacy was killed. The plaque was unveiled by the National Graves Association in 1937, in the presence of a huge crowd of onlookers.

Following Irish independence, the renaming of streets became commonplace in Dublin. In the decades following independence, members of a wide variety of nationalist organisations would call for the renaming of that street to honour Seán Treacy.

Among the organisations demanding the changing of the name Talbot Street in the 1940s were Ailtirí na hAiséirghe, a fascist movement whose name translated into 'Architects of the Resurrection' and who were led by

Gearóid Ó Cuinneagáin. The politics of the movement very much fused European fascism with a deep sense of Irish Christianity and cultural nationalism. In their 1943 General Election leaflet outlining principal points of policy, the organisation noted that: 'Your duty to Ireland does not end with the casting of your vote. Serve Ireland always. Speak the language. Encourage others to speak the language. Help everything Irish and national and clean!'

On 1 November 1943, members of *Ailtirí na hÁiseirghe* created uproar at a meeting of Dublin Corporation by shouting from the public galleries while the Corporation was sitting. At the time of the interruptions, the Corporation was discussing the planned removal of Queen Victoria's statue from Leinster House. One man rose and shouted: 'Get rid of all the symbols of slavery in the streets! We demand that Talbot Street be renamed Seán Treacy Street. Young Ireland is awakening.'

It was reported that another member of the group shouted: 'Honour Seán Treacy, despite the shopkeepers of Talbot Street. If you do not, you are not worthy of the name of Irishmen.' Following their interruptions, the men began to file out, loudly chanting '*Éire aiseirghe, Aiseirghe abú!*'

On 6 April 1944, a letter appeared in the *Irish Independent* in which it was noted that:

When passing down Talbot Street the other day I was surprised to see the printed words: "*Sraid*

Sean Ui Threasaigh" [Seán Treacy Street] high up on the wall, pasted over the ordinary Talbot Street name-plate. As I have not heard of any indication recently that Dublin Corporation has sanctioned the changing of the name of Talbot Street I was astonished to see the change already carried out.

The writer noted that three days prior the *Irish Press* had actually written of an event occurring on 'Seán Treacy Street', a street that on paper didn't exist! 'I wonder if this sentence was written as a result of some knowledge of official approval for the change?' the writer asked.

The paper noted in response to the letter that a recent Corporation meeting had passed a motion urging a change of name, and that it now required only the support of the majority of rent payers on Talbot Street. Ultimately, the rent payers of the street voted by an overwhelming majority not to rename the street, which led to considerable controversy.

The *Irish Press* objected strongly to this move by the rent payers, and noted that street names in Dublin had long been used to commemorate people like:

The Rutlands, the Mountjoys, the Brunswicks, the Ormondes, the Talbots and the rest – these are not names that we remember with any particular pride, though it may be useful to preserve one or two as a reminder of the historic past.'

It was found that most rent payers who voted against the name had done so on two grounds. Firstly, the belief that the name 'Seán Treacy Street' would lead to some confusion with the nearby Sean MacDiarmada Street; and secondly the belief that the proposed name should be shortened to 'Treacy Street' alone. No such compromise was ever reached however.

At their annual conference in October 1944, the Gaelic League passed a motion in which they called for the trade union movement, the Old IRA, the GAA and other nationalist organisations to boycott the shops of Talbot Street as 'they were showing disrespect to the memory of Seán Treacy and all those who believed in national freedom.' In reality, however, of the 100 plus business premises in the area, the name change had been defeated by a vote of 30 to 3.

The campaign to rename the street continued well into the 1950s, and in October 1955 it was reported in *The Irish Times* that:

> In broad daylight, often during the busy lunch hour period, multi-coloured Sraid Ui Treasaig posters are being pasted on hoardings and house-corners in Dublin's Talbot Street. A member of one of several political organisations anxious to see the name of the street changed to Seán Treacy Street said: 'The posters are put up when the street is at its busiest. No one takes any notice of them then. If the posters were put up at night we might get arrested.'

Efforts to rename the street Seán Treacy Street, or even Treacy Street, ultimately failed. While several streets in the vicinity have seen name changes in the decades following independence, Talbot Street has remained the same.

44.

Lenny Bruce's whirlwind trip to Dublin

Lenny Bruce, the critically influential American stand-up comic and social critic, visited Dublin just once in his lifetime.

His 26-hour stopover in the city played a central role in an amazing saga that saw the comedian deported from London twice in less than a week in 1963.

Banned in nineteen American States for his 'obscene' language and anti-establishment routines, he had been deported by British authorities just after arriving at Heathrow Airport in April 1963.

Not one to give up that easily, a daring plan was drawn up by friends in London to smuggle him into England via Ireland.

Bruce arrived into Dublin Airport on board an Aer Lingus Boeing Shamrock Jet, from New York, at 2:30 p.m. on Good Friday, April 1963. Here, he told Irish officials a story that he had earlier arrived into Ireland via Shannon Airport and that he was cleared through their US immigration desk before boarding an internal flight to Dublin.

Waiting for him at Dublin Airport was Peter Bellwood, a young Belfast-born, London-based writer and performer, whose only job was to get Bruce back to London, where he was to perform at The Establishment – London's first satire club.

Bruce stayed over with Peter on Good Friday in the luxurious Gresham Hotel on Dublin's O'Connell Street. Little is known about Bruce's one and only night in Dublin besides the fact that he spent a lengthy time searching for a tailor's that was open to get his favourite suit repaired. In the early hours of Easter Saturday, the two drove to Belfast in a hired car with the intention of flying domestic to Heathrow Airport.

Things, however, did not go to plan. While he did make it to London, plain-clothes policemen arrested him that afternoon and he was imprisoned overnight in a police station near the airport until the Home Office eventually got the necessary paperwork together to deport him once again.

That week of events, in which Dublin played an integral role, had many consequences.

The Establishment, financially ruined from the lost income and heavy legal fees spent fighting Bruce's deportation, closed its doors for good in September of that year. Lenny Bruce, shook up and depressed over the double rejection and deportation from Britain, succumbed to heroin once again – his first score in months. With the subsequent publicity from his London double deportation, more US venues banned or cancelled his shows as legal pressures mounted to keep Lenny Bruce from performing live.

Arrested yet again for obscenity while playing in the Cafe Au Go Go in New York in April 1964, the following six month trail remains one of the most famous and controversial court cases regarding American censorship since the days of McCarthyism. Bruce was sentenced, on 21 December 1964, to four months in a workhouse. Fortunately he was freed on bond during the appeal against his conviction.

Before an appeals decision was made, however, Bruce was found dead, naked in the bathroom of his Hollywood Hills home with a syringe sticking out of his arm. The official cause of death, which occurred on 3 August 1966, was 'acute morphine poisoning caused by an accidental overdose.' He was 40 years old.

In December 2003, 37 years after his death, New York Governor George Pataki granted Bruce a posthumous pardon for his obscenity conviction.

Thanks to Sideline Productions for the initial research for this story.

45.

The Free Peace Festival of 1978

The Free Peace Festival, which took place in the Phoenix Park in 1978, can be seen either as a bitter disappointment or as a fantastic achievement, depending on your outlook.

It can be seen as a disappointment, for it was supposed to take place over a full weekend, feature over 90 acts over three stages and attract over 50,000 revellers, but in the end, the festival opened with only one stage, a handful of bands and only 3,000 or so fans.

The achievement lies that in the fact that a free festival took place in the Phoenix Park that attracted 3,000 people, three times more than the year before.

Bill 'Ubi' Dywer (1933–2001), the eccentric Irishborn self-described 'non-violent anarchist' and main organiser, made his name running the Windsor Free Festival in London from 1972–1974, which saw over 100,000 attend and was widely seen as being the forerunner for the Free Festival Movement and more directly the Stonehenge Free Festival and the later Glastonbury Festival.

The 1978 festival in the Phoenix Park was supposed to feature over 90 acts including U2, De Dannan, Clannad, Horslips, Paul Brady, The Bach St Kids, VHF, Biros, Revolver, Rocky De Valera & The Gravediggers and Brown Thomas. It's unclear which of these actually played in the end. As well as music, there was theatre, mime and an adventure playground for children.

Gareth Byrne remembers that day:

Saturday 5 August the first morning was bright when organisers began to arrive at The Hollow. The first band played to a trickle of spectators. By midday I spotted half a dozen individuals in wheelchairs at one corner, supervised helpfully by Fergus Rowan and a friend, who had arranged special transport. Gradually the attendance swelled to a few hundred individuals and parents with children. More bands arrived and got their gear ready. By lunchtime the sky had clouded over and there was a heavy downpour. Ubi donned a yellow showerproof cape and put a cheerful face on things by dancing and twirling to the music around the bandstand. I noticed a sharp row he had with members of one band who got nervous about the possibility of electric shock and wanted to switch off the AC/DC system. He effed and blinded loudly at them and insisted that the show go on. The shower died down, the sun reappeared, and Ubi disappeared. More people turned up to listen and the music went on smoothly until about 7 p.m.

Around 4 p.m. Ubi reappeared at the
bandstand and looked the worse for drink. His
reeking breath and raving demeanour suggested
several double shots of Irish whiskey in addition
to the customary pints of Guinness. A uniformed
member of the Gardaí (police) and a plain-
clothes detective tried to reason with him. He
was escorted from The Hollow, somehow got
to the ferry harbour at Dun Laoghaire and took
the boat and overnight train to London. British
newspapers reported a week later that Thames
Valley police arrested him as he arrived at Windsor
Park intending to launch a banned free music
festival there. He was sentenced to jail and didn't
return to Dublin until the autumn of 1979.

In many ways, the Free Peace Festival was overshad-
owed by the first Carnsore Anti-Nuclear Rally, which
took place just two weeks later and attracted over
10,000 people. It saw Christy Moore, Andy Irvine,
Mick Hanly, Paddy Glackin, Jimmy Crowley, Bothy
Band, Al O'Donnell, Red Peters, Sacre Bleu, Stagalee,
Midnight Well, Seamus Creagh, Jackie Daly, Clannad
and Barry Moore (before he came Luka Bloom) take to
the stage. It was also the first gig of classic Dublin New
Wave band The Atrix.

Ubi later ran as an independent in Dun Laoghaire
for the Dáil in 1981 and 1982, receiving 927 and
418 votes respectively, and later was involved in the

campaigning for legalisation of cannabis and H-Block's prisoner rights. He was involved in a cycling accident in the late 1990s in the Dublin Mountains, never fully recovered from his injuries and died at the age of 68 in 2001.

46.

No sex shops please, we're Irish!

Adult shops dot the streets of the capital today, but the earliest such shops in Ireland caused huge contention and led to street protest and opposition from those in authority. As late as 1999, with the opening of Ann Summers on O'Connell Street, newspapers found it necessary to ask what the men who occupied the General Post Office across the street in 1916 would have thought.

Prior to Dublin's earliest adult shop, and often mistaken for it, there had been Yvonne Costello's store Kinks in the 1980s: a lingerie shop that carried some 'novelty items', but never went far enough as to bring the force of conservative elements knocking on the door. Costello was of course a former Miss Ireland, and a character with whom the media held some fascination. Kinks was about as risqué as things were to get in Dublin or the South for some time, and while adult shops thrived north of the border, they were yet to land in the capital. Kinks on South Anne Street even featured in the weekend supplement of *The Irish Times*, and while widely remembered by Dubs as the first sex shop in Dublin, this labelling just doesn't suit.

Frank Young, owner of the Belfast sex shop Private Lines, was interviewed by the *Sunday Independent* in February of 1991 about his intentions to bring the store to the sexually conservative heart of the Republic. Young, the paper noted, 'looks more like an accountant than someone who sells sex for a living', and in his interview he said that many of his customers were coming from across the border anyway, making a move into Dublin logical in his eyes. Responsible for the *Esprit* and *Excel* magazines, which were subject to censorship south of the border, Young believed that were it not for the two menaces of 'raving feminists and various Christian groups', the magazine would have a circulation on the island to rival the *Sunday World*. There was, Young insisted, a strong desire for adult shops further south than Newry. Belfast's first sex shop had opened in 1982, with huge pickets from Christian groups making the owners of 'Mr Dirty Books' perfectly aware they were unwelcome on the Castlereagh Road!

When sex shops did ultimately land in the Republic later on in the 1990s, few could have predicted the backlash. As Diarmaid Ferriter wrote in his history of the Irish and their sexuality, *Occasions of Sin*, these shops on one level represented the normalisation of sexuality 'by its being transformed into a commodity', but to others this was very much a threat to the very moral fibre that held our society together. Jim

Bellamy, an Aberdeen native, was responsible for the earliest sex shops in the south, opening Utopia outlets in Bray, Dublin, Dundalk and Limerick in very quick succession. In Limerick, one protestor told *The Irish Times* that 'paedophiles and other sex perverts feed off these kind of places', but the sales figures suggested that Jim Bellamy's store held a wide appeal to the general public. Thousands joined 'pray-ins' against Bellamy's shop in Limerick and throughout the Province, organised by the 'Solidarity' movement. *The Irish Times'* image of Mr Bellamy, standing alongside a mannequin in a maid's outfit, must be one of the most unusual images the paper has ever printed. Bellamy's Bray outlet, opened late in 1991, was the first sex shop in the Republic. I don't suppose we'll ever see a plaque upon the site.

When Utopia made the short journey into the Irish capital in 1993, it arrived on Capel Street, today home to more sex shops than any other street in Dublin. Utopia, however, was about to become Utophia. While the sign writing tradition is sadly dying out in Dublin today, and hand painted shopfronts are few and far between, a painter was given the honour of putting the name above the door of Dublin's first sex shop. Incredibly, and in the spirit of a good Dublin story, he spelt it wrongly, and Utophia was born, as it was to remain.

Dublin's early sex shops found themselves in a very unusual place, coming head to head with the rather extreme censorship laws still in place at the time.

While inflatable people and inflatable sheep were both harmless enough in the eyes of the state, the printed word and image still posed the greatest threat to the moral decency of a people. As Bellamy was to tell Sean Moncrieff in a 1994 interview for *The Irish Times*, what we had was 'four old men and a judge deciding the morals of the country'. Throughout 1995, the shops were raided on numerous occasions by customs officers and Gardaí in relation to the selling of indecent or obscene materials, in the form of video tapes. In many cases such materials were returned to the shops afterwards when they were deemed to be within the law. This situation saw Bellamy take court proceedings to challenge the decision of the authorities to raid his stores with such frequency.

Heading into the mid 1990s, Utophia was joined by Condom Power, Miss Fantasia and other outlets, which remain in Dublin to this day, ironically rather recession proof despite the early controversies around them. Remarkably, by the late 1990s, another scandal would blow up with the opening of Ann Summers on O'Connell Street.

It says a great deal about Dubliners today that more of us are offended by the ugly and plentiful 'temporary signs' and ill-thought-out shopfronts on our main thoroughfare than what is essentially a lingerie store, but in 1999 Ann Summers found itself in hot water over its chosen Dublin location. It would take a High Court challenge to secure the future of the shop, with

Ann Summers informed by Dublin Corporation that their use of the premises and their range of products were unacceptable and in conflict with the objectives of the O'Connell Street Integrated Area Plan.

47.

The Viking – Dublin's first Gay pub?

The Viking Inn, at 75 Dame Street, predated The George as Dublin's first 'exclusively gay bar', according to some. Situated just beside the Olympia Theatre, the pub was taken over and renamed Brogan's Bar in the early 1990s.

The earliest newspaper records show that 75 Dame Street operated first as a surgery for a 'mechanical dentist' by the name of John Egar in the 1850s. Remodelled as a public house, it was known as O'Brien Bros. (1920s), Kerins (1940s), McCabes (1950s), Leonards (1960s–1970s), The Crampton Court (late 1970s), The Viking Inn (1979–1987), The City Hall Inn (1989–1993) and finally Brogan's Bar (1993–present).

The Viking was the first bar in the city to be owned by a gay proprietor and to be opened specifically as a gay bar. It closed in 1987, shortly after The Parliament (now The Turk's Head) opened and a full two years after The George first set up shop. Commenter PM said it 'was tiny and very poserish … like a gay version of The Bailey!'

Poster 'John K.' on gaire.com remembers:

Because it was beside the Olympia, there were many amusing incidents when straight people, especially from the country, went in and quickly began to feel very uncomfortable ... The Viking was a great spot. I first went in there around 1980 [and] I have no recollection of any Garda harassment.

Another poster 'Fourcort' recalls plucking up the courage to visit the place for the first time:

One night in the early eighties, I walked the entire length of Dame St. about 20 times trying to get up the courage to push in through the door of The Viking. A couple of drag queens cottoned on to me at one stage and started laughing at me. Eventually, I just forced myself in, got a pint (I never drink pints, I just thought I could make it last, and not have to move again), and went and hid down the back.

Tony O'Connell, who commented on our blog article, refutes the claim, originally made by gay historian Tonie Walsh, that The Viking was Dublin's first exclusively gay bar:

The Viking was not the first exclusively gay bar. Bartley Dunne's and Rice's were the first 'gay' bars for me in the mid sixties. The Viking opened later. For obvious legal reasons neither Rice's nor Dunne's could profess to be gay. Barry Dunne described his clientele as 'avant garde'! When The Viking opened it became a stopping point on the 'pilgrimage' between Rice's and Dunne's.

I have great memories of The Viking, in particular a manager named Pat who, although not gay, was so supportive and helpful to a degree that I have not come across in a gay bar anywhere in Ireland since.

The original blog article prompted Aidan Coyle to leave this comment:

I remember the Viking with great affection as it was a regular haunt for me and my mates in 1985–87 during my student years when I first ventured out. I can also remember folk wandering in en route to the Olympia next door. It was really funny to see them come in and then watch the dawning realisation that this wasn't the sort of hostelry they were expecting it to be. I recall that some of my mates were George people and I was definitely a Viking person but for the life of me I can't remember what the difference between them was. It feels rather odd to see my youthful socialising places being considered part of history already.

48.

The Bowl of Light

Much like the 'Time in the Slime' and the 'Floozie in the Jacuzzi', the 'The Tomb of the Unknown Gurrier' is remembered with a smile by Dubliners of a certain age. The Bowl of Light on O'Connell Bridge was barely in place before coming under attack, and was the subject of ridicule from the very beginning, with even Myles na gCopaleen taking aim at the public ornament.

The Bowl was the centrepiece of the *An Tóstal* scheme of decorations on the O'Connell Bridge in 1953. The *An Tóstal* event was an annual festival, which ran from 1953 to 1958, aimed at promoting Ireland as a tourist destination, and also luring Irish exiles home to re-engage with the country. It was, quite simply, to be a celebration of Irish culture and traditions at home. In April 1952, a report in *The Irish Times* gave some idea of the ambition of the project, noting that 'the Board stressed that while *An Tóstal* would be based in Dublin, it would be of national interest. It will be intended that the whole country will, for the period of three weeks, be at home to Irish exiles and friends from everywhere.'

Major-General Hugo MacNeill was appointed organiser of *An Tóstal*. On the eve of the event, he wrote that:

In a few days the flag of *An Tóstal* will be hoisted ceremoniously all over Ireland, and the Easter fires blazing on the hills of Ireland will illuminate the skies with the message of IRELAND AT HOME!

The event would see the erection of ornaments and public art throughout the capital, but no piece captured the attention of the public quite like 'The Bowl Of Light', owing primarily to the fact it was to be a permanent feature. The Bowl was described in *The Irish Times* as:

A copper bowl, with a diameter of about 4 feet, is fitted to a semi-circular bridge of tubular girders which spans an octagonal basin, measuring about 15 ft. by 18 ft. and containing about a foot depth of water. The many coloured plastic 'flames', which could revolve, were set in the bowl, and at night were illuminated from the inside.

The Bowl was erected behind hoardings so that the public were unable to see what was to be placed on the bridge. In the region of 3,000 people gathered on Saturday 3 April 1953 to see the unveiling of 'The Bowl Of Light', around which there was great curiosity among the public.

The *Irish Independent* reported that things turned ugly on the Saturday night, as Gardaí struggled to free traffic lanes and found themselves having to draw their batons against the large crowd. The paper noted that: 'In scenes which followed floral decorations were thrown at

Gardaí and windows were broken in a number of shops in O'Connell Street, including Clery's. About 12 arrests were made.'

It was reported by the *Sunday Independent* that 'at no time did the force of Gardaí on duty appear adequate to deal with the disturbance.'

While there was widespread bemusement at 'The Bowl Of Light', it would become one of Dublin's most short-lived public ornaments. On 19 April, only weeks after its unveiling, the 'flames' from the Bowl were chucked into the River Liffey, the actions of Anthony Wilson, a young student of Trinity College Dublin.

Wilson had been at a party, which was described in the courts of law as 'a particularly good party.' Following it, he and friends went around the city enjoying themselves, and were spotted standing on the O'Connell Bridge complete with umbrellas, despite it being a fine day. The students made speeches there to the public, and it was evidently clear to those who heard them that a fair amount of alcohol had been consumed. 'Wilson could not explain how he came to take the light and throw it into the river.'

Witnesses described seeing a young man climb upon the parapet of the basin, pull the flames from the bowl and make his way towards the parapet of the bridge, hurling the plastic flames into the river. The young man made a run for it, but was caught on Aston's Quay. Newspaper reports noted that some members of the crowd had shouted 'Throw him in the river!' at Gardaí following his arrest. The student was ordered to pay £48 7/6 to cover the damage.

The Bowl attracted its fair share of detractors in the letters pages of the national newspapers. None, however, were as loud in their criticisms as Myles na gCopaleen, who lambasted the Bowl and the *Tóstal* event itself. On 9 April 1953, Myles wrote tongue-incheek of those who had been responsible for the scenes at O'Connell Bridge on the Saturday:

> I did not have the pleasure to be in Dublin last Saturday night but absence did not deny me a glow of pride when I learnt what the citizens did when the pubs closed at ten. They decided to give the odd gawking visitor a real Irish welcome ... Here we had Cathleen Ni Hooligan in person.

He went on to attack the Bowl, writing that it was:

> ... an appalling piece of ironwork bearing a basin out of which emerges a 'plastic flame'. This metal thing has a spout on it, and the original intention was to have a 'fountain' on the bridge. Nothing will ever in our time come out of that spout, but how much of the ratepayers cash has gone up it for this change of 'plan'? No need to guess. The figure is £1,768.

With its flames now long in the river, the Bowl continued to cause controversy through 1953 and into

1954. It is perhaps most commonly remembered among Dubliners today as 'The Tomb of the Unknown Gurrier'. The late Basil Payne would pen an excellent epitaph for the 'Tomb of the Unknown Gurrier', writing that:

> The City Fathers' grim myopia
> confines me to this non-U-topia;
> to reinforce their sentiment
> They buried me in thick cement.

49.

Dublin's shortest street

For many years, the shortest street in Dublin was Canon Street, once situated just off Bride Street near Saint Patrick's Cathedral. It was originally named Petty Canon Alley in the 1750s after the minor canons (members of the clergy who 'assist in the daily services of a cathedral, but are not members of the chapter') of Saint Patrick's Cathedral.

The street had just one address, the public house of Messrs Rutledge and Sons, and was thus described in 1949 as the 'shortest street in the world' (the *Irish Press*), and in 1954 as the 'shortest street in Europe' (*The Irish Times*).

The pub was demolished, and the street disappeared along with it in the late 1960s to make way for the widening of Bride Street.

Today, it is not as clear which street in Dublin is the shortest.

One possible contender is Palace Street, just off Dame Street and attached to Dame Lane. It is certainly very small, and only has three addresses (the third being very much a recent one).

No.1 is the French restaurant Chez Max, and No.2 was the building that hosted the The Sick and Indigent Roomkeepers Society from 1855 to 1992, while

The compact Palace Street, off Dame Street. (Paul Reynolds)

Kevin Street Cross near St Patrick's Cathedral. (Paul Reynolds)

No.3, only built in 1999, hosts the Corporate Services Department of Dublin City Council.

Another possibility is Cross Kevin Street, which connects Bride Street with New Bride Street, between the junctions of those two streets with Bishop Street and Lower Kevin Street. However, it cannot really be described as a street any more. Its houses and shops were demolished some time ago when the road widened. It is now merely a crossroads.

The final option is Dean Street, which links to The Coombe and Upper Kevin Street. It only has four addresses. It certainly is very short, but I think Palace Street just nicks it.

50.

A Stout and Handy Man; Dan Donnelly

Ye sons of proud Britannia, your boasting now
    give o'er,
Since by our hero Donnelly, your hero is no
    more;
In eleven rounds he got nine knocks down,
    besides broke his jawbone,
Shake hands, says she, brave Donnelly, the battle
    is our own.

>   – From the ballad 'Donnelly and Cooper'

Irish history is rich in stories of playwrights and poets whose own characters match if not outshone their talent with a pen. O'Casey, Behan, O'Brien; arguably tales of their exploits exceed those of their creations. When it comes to sports people, we are arguably equally rich in these characters, and one name that comes to mind is Dan Donnelly, a knighted prizefighter who won the hearts and minds of Irish men and women in the early nineteenth century.

With Ireland still under colonial British rule, and with ten years yet to pass until the uprising of 1798, Dan Donnelly was born into poverty in a house on Townsend Street in the heart of Dublin's Docklands. His father died at an early age, and Dan trained as a carpenter in order to support his family. He grew to be a formidable beast of a man, standing six foot and one half inch tall and weighing over 14 stone. As scary as he looked, by all accounts he was a pleasant man, and a man of manners, on more than one occasion stepping in to stop muggings and assaults around the area of Townsend Street. Stories say his introduction to boxing came from fighting, and beating, a bullying English sailor in a bar close to his home. Another story tells of him carrying the corpse of an old lady who had died, impoverished and alone, to a local graveyard and 'convincing' two gravediggers who were at work that the hole they were digging was to be her final resting place.

While carpentry was his trade, it was with his fighting prowess that he excelled, quickly garnering a reputation as one of Ireland's best fighters. Coupled with his sheer bulk, in boxing terms, his reach, or the length of his arms, was believed to be unnaturally long for his height. His infamy as a bare-knuckle boxer grew, and he was soon picked up by trainer Captain William Kelly, and he progressed from brawls outside taverns to organised fights, with a considerable purse to be taken home by the victor.

The fight for which he is most remembered was his second, which took place on 13 December 1815 in

The Curragh, County Kildare against British champion George Cooper. Now called Donnelly's Hollow, the area was a natural amphitheatre with sloping hillsides surrounding a flat area of ground where the fight took place. It is said that over 30,000 people made the trek to Kildare for the fight by foot and carriage, with the upper classes mixing with slum dwellers, the majority of whom had a stake on the outcome.

The fight itself was said to be a dour affair, with the favourite, Cooper (1/10 to win) using dirty tactics and falling to his knees on a number of occasions in order to get rounds to be stopped. Donnelly put paid to the Englishman's arrogance when he broke his jaw with a right hook in the eleventh round, taking the fight in the process. Cooper tried to get Donnelly disqualified, as he had fallen on his knee again when Donnelly struck, but the victory was declared by acclaim from the crowd.

Donnelly's victory against Cooper was seen as a national event; an Irish peasant not only beating, but embarrassing the British champion at the height of the Empire. His trip back to Dublin is said to have taken over two weeks, so many were his stops, doing his best to spend the £60 purse he earned from the fight in taverns along the way. His footsteps from the Hollow itself are still there to be seen, as supporters, keen to follow in his footsteps, did so physically, marking out the steps on the landscape, as people still do to this day. A stone obelisk marks the spot where the fight took place, bearing the inscription 'Dan Donnelly beat Cooper on this spot 13th Dec. 1815.'

Donnelly eventually made his way to England, where he became parlour entertainment for the wealthy upper classes who welcomed him at their parties. It was at one of these parties that Donnelly (according to legend, as there is no documentation to prove so) knelt before the Prince Regent George IV and was granted knighthood with a sword tap on each shoulder – an Irish pugilist who once worked with the brother of Anne Devlin, a figure central to Robert Emmet's revolt of 1803 receiving knighthood from a future King of England. As implausible as it seems; it is apparently true.

He moved back to Ireland, and with the money he had earned from his fights, and with his reputation still intact, he decided to go into business, opening four bars in succession. But, as is often the case, he was the bar's best customer and this was eventually his undoing. Of all the bars, Fallon's Capstan Bar is the only one that remains in business today. He died broke and lonely on 18 February 1820 at the young age of 32.

A funeral procession of over 50,000 followed his coffin, and he was buried in Bully's Acre: a pauper's graveyard in Kilmainham, and one of Dublin's oldest. Within days, his body was stolen by grave robbers; riots broke out in Dublin upon the news and Surgeon Hall, who had purchased the body, returned Donnelly to his grave in Bully's Acre – minus his right arm. The arm was transported to Edinburgh University, where it was used in anatomy lessons, was taken around England by a travelling circus, was brought back to Ireland and displayed in several pubs throughout the twentieth century, and went to New York and back before it found its resting place in The Hideout Bar, Kilcullen where it remained on show until 2006.

Blackwood's magazine, a conservative British miscellany of poetry and creative writing published since the early nineteenth century, ran the following epitaph in a collection of poems in July 1821. It is dedicated to 'Sir Daniel Donnelly,' giving some credence at least to the idea that the bare-knuckle pugilist from Dublin's inner city slums did indeed kneel in front of a young George IV a pauper, but rose a knight.

Underneath this pillar high,
Lies Sir Daniel Donnelly;
He was a stout and handy man,
And people called him buffing Dan.
Knighthood he took from George's sword,
And well he wore it by my word!
He died at last, from forty-seven
Tumblers of punch he drank one even.
O'erthrown by punch, unharm'd by fist,
He died an unbeaten pugilist.
Such a buffer as Donnelly,
Ireland never again will see.

51.

Paddy Clare: The man who took sabbatical to fight Franco

Mark O'Brien in his 2001 book *De Valera, Fianna Fáil and the Irish Press* makes fleeting reference to an *Irish Press* reporter named Paddy Clare, who 'took sabbatical leave' in order to join the International Brigade during the Spanish Civil War.

Immediately, I became fond of this chap who decided to take a 'leave of absence' from work, not to go on holiday but to join the International Brigade and risk his life in the defence of the Second Spanish Republic.

A bit of digging unearthed that Clare was firstly a lifelong Irish republican who fought in both the War of Independence and in the Civil War on the Anti-Treaty side, and secondly an individual who has largely been forgotten.

Born in Dublin into a republican family in 1908, his father Mick was an old Fenian. Joining Na Fianna Éireann in his early teens, he saw action in Dublin during the War of Independence. Following the Treaty, he took the republican side in the Civil War and was a member of the Four Courts garrison in 1922. Subsequently, he was imprisoned in both Kilmainham and Mountjoy where, in the latter, he once went on hunger strike.

Always a keen writer, Clare contributed articles to *An Phoblacht* and *The Nation*. His work caught the eye of De Valera, who asked him to join the fledgling *Irish Press* in 1931. He would stay with the paper for the next 43 years, first as diary clerk, then a reporter and finally as 'night-town man'.

Still committed to Irish republican socialist politics, he made the decision to take a period of leave from the newspaper to join the International Brigade.

Unfortunately, that is all I know about his involvement in the Spanish Civil War. No one has been able to either confirm or deny whether he actually did see action in Spain.

Returning to Dublin and to the *Irish Press*, he was appointed as the paper's 'night-town' reporter, a post he'd keep until 1973. A tough job, Clare would man the office throughout the night and chase any leads or stories that occurred during the hours of darkness.

Clare passed away in 1983 at the age of 75. Tim-Pat Coogan wrote at the time:

Gravely voiced, indefatigably cheerful, with the yellow pallor of the night worker, which he was for scores of years, Paddy Clare, to generations of young *Irish Press* journalists, epitomised the ideal of the hard-shelled, heart-of-gold professional reporter.

An IRA veteran of at least two wars (possibly three) and a respected journalist of over forty years, Clare lived a full life.

52.

Flaunting censorship, Irish feminists and Spare Rib in Dublin

Spare Rib was a second-wave British feminist publication set up in 1972 to provide a feminist alternative to commercial women's magazines. It was very much a publication of the left, for example often writing critically of Britain's role in Ireland, along with giving coverage to labour disputes. The excellent study *Women and Journalism* notes that W.H. Smith refused to stock the first issue of the magazine, which contained such shocking content as a feature on skin care and an interview with George Best! It also included articles on sex, gender equality and women's role in history.

Quite unsurprisingly, the publication was banned in Ireland. In February of 1977, following a complaint to the Censorship of Publications Board, it was decided that the magazine was unfit for the eyes of the Irish public. A statement from the Board noted that having examined recent issues of the British magazine, the magazine was found to have been 'usually or infrequently indecent or obscene, and that for that reason the sale or distribution in the state of the said issues or future issues of the said periodical publication should be prohibited.'

Immediately following the banning of *Spare Rib*, there began a strong feminist campaign to overturn the ban. Ironically, while the magazine had enjoyed a miniscule readership in Ireland prior to the ban, the debate over the decision of the Censorship of Publications Board saw *Spare Rib* make its way into the letters pages of the national print media.

The secretary of Irishwomen United, an outspoken feminist organisation, would write to the editors of the national daily papers on 11 February 1977 stating that 'we see the censorship of *Spare Rib* as a direct attack of feminism and the women's movement.' Nell McCafferty would describe the organisation in a 1979 feature for *The Irish Times* as being 'composed, significantly, of trade unionists, professional women and the unemployed, who had scarcely heard of motherhood.'

Like large sections of the British left at the time, the people behind *Spare Rib* weren't entirely sure how to deal with matters relating to the island next door. Rose Ades, one of the women on the collective behind the publication, remarked that they did not wish to be seen to be imposing any sort of 'British cultural imperialism' and that 'we don't want to be thought of as foisting something essentially alien on Irish people if they don't want it.'

Yet Irish feminists did want it, and they were prepared to fight for it. Three days after the letter from Irishwomen United appeared in the national daily papers, on

A copy of *Spare Rib* magazine, openly sold on Dublin's streets by
feminists despite being banned (Fallon Collection)

Valentines Day, 20 members of the feminist organisation
boarded the 8 a.m. shopper's special train for Belfast
with the intention of returning with 150 copies of the
publication. As Nell McCafferty wrote at the time:

> The publishers of the magazine had donated the
> copies free and sent them over to Belfast as a con-
> tribution to the women's' struggle in the south.

The women intended to return to Dublin on the 5.30 p.m. train, depending of course on what happened to the banned magazine during Customs Inspection in Dundalk.

The women managed to bring the publication into the south with no opposition from Customs in Dundalk, and arrived at Connolly Station as planned that night, where the assembled media awaited the inevitable showdown with the Guardians of the Peace. In the end, three Gardaí approached the women, attempted to apprehend one, failed, and not a single copy of the publication was seized by the state.

Two weeks later, on 28 February, the organisation would challenge the law banning the publication by openly selling it on the streets of Dublin. A packed protest meeting at the Mansion House saw speakers denounce the ban, and three women told Gardaí formally that they intended to sell the publication there and then to all interested. They were Marie McMahon and Joanne O'Brien of Irishwomen United and Sue Burns of the Irish Family Planning Service. No attempt was made to stop them. Interestingly, Marie McMahon had been involved in the Hume Street occupation and the Irish Civil Rights Association.

On International Women's Day 1977, the Irishwomen United movement marched from Parnell Square to Stephen's Green in protest at the banning of the publication, before returning to Parnell Square to join a trade union demonstration against unemploment.

In the immediate aftermath of the banning of the publication in February of 1977, Marie McMahon was arrested for postering illegally for the prior mentioned protest meeting. Questioned under the Emergency Powers Act and appearing in court twice in 1977, she was bound to the peace and if she refused to sign the peace bond she would face seven days' imprisonment. She refused, but it was not until March of 1980 that she would be arrested and imprisoned. Almost three years on from her initial arrest, her imprisonment angered many and saw protests organised outside Mountjoy Prison.

Interestingly, *Spare Rib* made its way into the Irish media on several occasions for its coverage of Irish affairs and also for its reporting by Irish migrant women in Britain. *The Irish Press* of 11 June 1980, for example, wrote of its *Off The Boat* feature, which spoke to Siobhan and Mary Lennon, two Irish women living in England, about their experiences. The feature spoke about the 'PFI' phenomenon, 'PFI' standing for 'Pregnant From Ireland'. One woman was reported as saying to *Spare Rib* 'I couldn't stay in Ireland what with the stigma of being an unmarried mother'. Women also spoke about anti-Irish racism in Britain at the height of the troubles.

In October of 1982, *Spare Rib* released an issue that focused primarily on Ireland, at that stage of course a pressing issue for the British left, with the situation in the north as it was. The issue featured prominent Irish feminists such as Nell McCafferty and figures like Anne Connolly of the Well Woman Clinic in Dublin. It had a strong anti-imperialist feel too, with articles focusing on the situation in Armagh women's prison alongside a review of Nora Connolly O'Brien's *We Shall Rise Again.* *Spare Rib*'s strong line on Northern Ireland remained the same throughout the 1980s, with the outlawing of strip searches a particular cause championed by the publication. The magazine would cease publication in 1993, but its influence cannot be overstated.

53.

The dangerous pastime of swimming in the Liffey

Jumping into the River Liffey has been a dangerous pastime for Dubliners for centuries. Some do it for kicks, some for bets and others just to cool down during hot summer days. A quick scan of the newspaper archives showcases the long-running (and often deadly) activity.

An article in *The Irish Times* from 29 March 1890 relates the story of a Miss Marie Finny, 'a professional swimmer' who was arrested just before she attempted to jump into the river off O'Connell Bridge.

In July 1909, a hotel porter called Hugh Bernard McGrath was rescued from the Liffey after he got into difficulty swimming after jumping from the eastern parapet of O'Connell Bridge.

A 'strange affair' was reported in 1932, which concerned an 'unknown man' who was seen swimming in the Liffey late one Monday evening. It was reported that he did not 'take any notice' of two life buoys that were thrown towards him or a boat that passed. He soon got into difficulty and drowned.

In August 1939, a soldier named James Donlan, 25, 'disappeared' while swimming in the Liffey. It took an extensive search operation to find his body.

The body of Michael Kinsella, 35, a labourer in the Guinness brewery, was found in the Liffey in November 1954. It was believed that he entered the river 'to settle a wager'.

There were also cases of young men drowning in the Liffey in August 1968, January 1977 and December 1986.

In May 1994, a Scottish tourist drowned after trying to swim across the Liffey in the early hours of a Saturday morning.

As a quick YouTube search can illustrate, jumping into the Liffey is as popular as ever.

Come Here To Me! does not recommend it.

54.

UCD in Sudan

University College Dublin (UCD) AFC's summer tour to Africa in 1980 was one that saw the college soccer club make the national headlines for all the wrong reasons at home. The tour would be remembered primarily for events in Khartoum, where a riot broke out in a stadium packed with 30,000 Sudanese fans. They had come to watch Merikh take on the Dubliners, and a goal from UCD was enough to send them into riot mode.

The UCD summer tour of 1980 was originally planned to just take on Kenyan opposition. The Sudan Football Association approached the side in the days leading up to their planned trip, however, and as such the trip was extended to include fixtures there. Kenyan side Abaluhya were first up against the students on 30 July. UCD would play six games in Kenya. They came out on top once, drew twice and lost three times.

The match on 14 August 1980 in Khartoum had been tense from very early on, as the captain of the local side had been sent off for a bad foul. From that point on the Irish squad were pelted with stones and bottles. Dr Tony O'Neill, manager of the students, told the *Irish Press* however that it was not until the students scored soon afterwards that all hell broke loose. David Cassidy was the goal scorer:

> The crowd seemed to go mad. They take their soccer very seriously here, and but for the timely intervention of the security forces to protect us the scene would have become very nasty indeed. When the police moved in, brandishing machine-guns and throwing tear-gas into the crowd to disperse them, our players were escorted to their dressing-room and afterwards back to the Hilton Hotel.

The referee was hospitalised as a result of the crowd trouble. Following the clash, referees in Sudan would strike, demanding greater protection during games, where such clashes had occurred before. Unsurprisingly, UCD cancelled their final planned game in Sudan! UCD's next clash was away to Drogheda United in the League Cup. They crashed out three-nil, and there was no violent disorder.

55.

Dublin's oldest hotel

Which is Dublin's oldest functioning hotel? A decent pub quiz question if I ever heard one.

Finding out the answer was harder than you might think. Google brought up a whole range of contradictory answers.

The Ormond Quay Hotel was described as 'Dublin's oldest hotel', The Gresham as 'Ireland's oldest hotel', The Shelbourne as the 'oldest hotel in Dublin', Wynn's as 'Dublin city centre's oldest hotel' and The Castle Hotel as 'the oldest hotel in Dublin'. No doubt many hotels in the city would love to claim the title!

The Ormond (Quay) Hotel, which closed in 2005, was 'only' opened in 1900.

Wynn's on Upper Abbey Street, where the decision to set up the Irish Volunteers took place in 1913, was established in 1845.

The Shelbourne on Saint Stephen's Green, which many people may think is Dublin's oldest hotel, opened its doors in 1824.

The Gresham Hotel on O'Connell Street stands a good chance, being established in 1817.

Is that the winner?

No, wait.

In fact it's the relatively unknown Castle Hotel on Great Denmark Street that deserves the title of being the oldest hotel in Dublin in continuous existence. It was opened by a Ms McCrory in 1809, a full eight years before The Gresham opened its doors.

The Castle Hotel was formerly a matching pair of Georgian houses, designed and built by John Ensor, with the stonework executed by Thomas Darley. Ensor was a pupil of Richard Castle, who had designed many of the great Irish houses including Russborough House and Leinster House. Upon the death of Castle, Ensor took over his practice and completed the Rotunda Hospital: the first ever lying-in hospital in Ireland.

The guest-house was first opened as the Norfolk Hotel, and then sold in the early 1900s and renamed The Leix Hotel. In 1930, it was up on the market again and bought by Donal O'Connor, who also acquired the two adjoining houses. In 1956, he amalgamated the entire four houses into the Castle Hotel.

Buswells (established in 1882) on Molesworth Street deserves an honourable mention. As does perhaps The Clarence on Wellington Quay, which, though completely renovated in 1992, was originally opened in 1852.

Then there are others like The Westbury (established in 1984), The Merrion (established in 1995) and The Westin (established in 2001), which I thought had been on the Dublin landscape for a lot longer.

56.

Marching to Dublin, Maynooth 1916

In 1966, the President of Maynooth College, the Right Reverend Monsignor Gerard Mitchell, invited the surviving members of an Irish Volunteers contingent who had marched from Maynooth to Dublin to partake in the 1916 Rising to the College. There, a mass took place celebrated by Father Tomhas O Fiaich, the Professor of Modern History at Maynooth.

It was a far cry from the last time some of those Volunteers had set foot in Maynooth College. In 1916, led by Domhnall Ua Buachalla (later the Governor General of the Free State), a group of local Volunteers found themselves in a very different situation. 'The movement', as far as the Irish Volunteers were concerned, was quite well organised in North Kildare, and Lieutenant Eamonn O' Kelly of the Volunteers arrived in Maynooth on Holy Thursday. He was aware of the plan for an insurrection on Easter Sunday, after being appointed to his position as a County Organiser by none other than Patrick Pearse.

O'Kelly had plans for the North Kildare Volunteers. He told Domhnall Ua Buachalla, the local leader of the force, to assemble his men on Easter Sunday in Maynooth town, and from there to proceed to Bodenstown Churchyard, to meet with other Kildare Volunteers. Writing of his memories of this in 1926 for *An tÓglách* magazine ('The Maynooth Volunteers In 1916'), Commandant Patrick Colgan noted that 'each man was asked if he was prepared to take part in the insurrection and each man agreed'.

Counter-orders caused confusion, and Colgan noted that no sooner had the men committed themselves to a Rising than word came through via a dispatch from Dublin that the mobilisation was called off. It would be Monday evening before they knew for sure that an insurrection was under way. The men were armed, though they didn't carry rifles, but rather single shotguns and roughly 40 rounds of ammunition.

'Many of us had never handled a gun prior to this, and much practising in the loading and unloading of our weapons now took place', Colgan would write. It was 7.15 p.m. on Easter Monday before the men left Maynooth. By this stage, the Rising was well under way in Dublin and key positions had been seized by the rebels. One of those who gathered in Maynooth was Thomas Byrne, known as 'Byrne the Boer'. He was a veteran of the Irish Brigade in the Boer War, having fought bravely alongside Major John MacBride. Byrne would have been one of the few men with military service in the group.

Before leaving Maynooth, the men proceeded through the main street to the College. Colgan noted that 'there were rumours to the effect that some of the students were anxious to join us', and the Volunteers also wanted to interview one of their own who had answered the original mobilisation call. 'Our quest for this employee brought us to the building occupied by the late Very Reverend J. Hogan, D.D., President of the College'. The President called on Domhnall O' Buachalla to return home and to see to it that his fellow Volunteers did the same. Undaunted, the men marched out the south-east gate of the College, and were now en route to Dublin.

The men proceeded to follow the Royal Canal to Leixlip, and from there take to the railway tracks. The men would march through Glasnevin Cemetery en route to the action, and Colgan noted that it was shortly after this point that they would encounter the first sign of the insurrection: two Volunteers armed with rifles on Cross Guns Bridge.

Making their way to the General Post Office, it was the face of James Connolly that would first greet the Maynooth men. 'We must have appeared as a motley crew of warriors to him, yet the welcoming smile which he gave us made us feel very full of ourselves'.

They were to provide relief to the Citizen Army men, who were surrounded at the *Evening Mail* office. Their journey there was nothing if not exciting, owing to the old man guarding the toll bridge. Demanding the toll, which the Volunteers did not have to hand, it was not until Lieutenant O' Kelly drew a revolver that the man capitulated. Later, when coming back to the southside of the city, Colgan noted that '… following the example set me by Lieutenant O' Kelly I presented my .32 revolver and received a free passage'.

These men had fallen into trouble, owing to the difficulties of the ICA at City Hall, where Captain Sean Connolly had fallen, and British forces had seized the Hall early on. City Hall had been abandoned, with William Oman of the ICA noting that on seeing the mobs in Werburgh Street 'cheering the troops', the men with him had decided that 'each man should take his chance individually in getting away'. He would ultimately end up in Jacob's, where a handful of other ICA men were to be found having retreated from Davy's pub at Portobello Bridge.

The Maynooth men who arrived on the scene then found themselves seizing the Exchange Hotel on Parliament Street. They themselves would come under fire from Dublin Castle. Patrick Colgan returned to the rebel HQ at the GPO to inform Connolly that only Domhnall O' Buachalla was armed with a rifle at the Hotel. Ultimately, it was only a matter of time until these men would end up back at the GPO, after a retreat up Temple Lane, which Colgan noted was the only time he had ever '… come near to breaking an athletic record'.

The men would assist in the defence of the General Post Office, and Patrick Colgan would later end up in

The Coliseum building on Sackville Street, but was to be captured on Liffey Street later. He described encountering an 'extremely decent' man named Boland, of Carlow, who he stated was somewhat sympathetic to the 'Finn Shaners', yet confused they had not waited until Irish men had returned from the War.

In 1966, Thomas Harris, Patrick Weafer, Timothy Tyrell, Joseph Ledwidge and Jack Maguire found themselves as guests in Maynooth College. Today, in the town square, a monument stands to them and the other men who assembled in Maynooth in 1916 to partake in the rebellion. Interestingly, the official report into the rebellion and its aftermath noted that there was now significant support for Irish separatists in Maynooth, something not present before the rebellion and executions of the leading figures. Domhnall Ua Buachalla would be elected a Sinn Féin TD for Kildare in 1918. The family hardware store in Maynooth, founded in 1853, remained in operation until 2005. Buckley's Lane is named after him today. Many of the other Maynooth men also remained active within the republican movement after being released following their roles in the Easter Rising.

57.

Favourite Dublin street name?

One of my favourite street names in Dublin is Lemon Street. It's more of a lane than a street, and is situated just off Grafton Street. It was named after Graham Lemon and his family, who owned property in the area. (It certainly has a better ring to it than its previous name: Little Grafton Street).

The Lemon family were the proprietors of The Confectioner's Hall on O'Connell Street; a beloved sweetshop for generations of Dubliners. Opening in 1842, it only closed its doors in 1984.

We recently asked our readers what their favourite street name in Dublin was. Here are some of the highlights:

Chick: 'The romantic in me just has to say 'Love Lane', off Lower Mount street.'

Elizabeth Bonass: 'George's Pocket, where I grew up'

DublinDilettante: 'My favourite is Tangier Lane. Such an incongruously evocative name for a skipfilled recess in Grafton St. round the back of the Gaiety.'

Skylarking: 'Gulistan Terrace. I assume there wasn't a Little Persia nestled in between Ranelagh and Rathmines at any stage.'

Ruth Gallagher: 'Blackpitts, Dublin 8. A great name and apparently where they buried plague victims in the Middle Ages.'

Colm Colm: 'Paradise Place, because it's anything but.'

Kevin Squires: 'Another vote for Fishamble St. I like to imagine in pre-historical times Lovecraftian fishpeople strolled up and down it all day. And Dalcassian Downs (mainly cos it sounds like a depressed race from Star Trek).'

Oisín Ó Ceallaigh: 'Lazer lane is a winner too'. *Franc Myles*: 'Hanover Lane off Francis Street, because it reminds me of the eighteenth century and because we archaeologists used to call it Hangover Lane in the late 80s.'

Fatti Burke: 'Fumbally Lane, basically because I have no clue what it means but it just sounds really onomatopoeic. The lane I fumble down.'

Ado Perry: 'MacGillamocholmog's Street as reported in Gilbert's History of Dublin. (Near High Street, apparently)'.

58.

Swastika Laundry
(1912–1987)

The Swastika Laundry operated from the Shelbourne Road in Ballsbridge, Dublin 4 for 75 years.

It was founded by John W. Brittain (1872–1937) from Manorhamilton, Co. Leitrim who was described by *The Irish Times* after his death as one of the 'pioneers of the laundry business in Ireland', having founded the Metropolitian and White Heather Laundries in 1899. He was also the owner of a famous horse called Swastika Rose, which was well known 'to frequenters of the Royal Dublin Society's Shows'.

The fact that people still talk about the laundry today is, for the most part, based on the fact that a swastika was used for their logo. However, it had absolutely no German or Nazi connections.

Peter Brittain, the grandson of John W. Brittain, was interviewed on the Derek Mooney programme in January 2008. He explained that his family chose the name because the swastika was a good luck symbol and that they had an ornamental cat, which had the emblem around its neck.

The laundry was founded in 1912, eight years before the German Nazi party decided to formally adopt the symbol. This important detail was emphasised by the company at the outbreak of the Second World War, when they changed the company's name to The Swastika Laundry (1912) to distance themselves from the NSDAP.

In his 1957 travel memoir *Irisches Tagebuch* (Irish Diary), the future Nobel Laureate Heinrich Böll recounts an unpleasant run-in with a Swastika Laundry van. He:

> … was almost run over by a bright-red panel truck, whose sole decoration was a big swastika. Had someone sold Völkischer Beobachter delivery trucks here, or did the Völkischer Beobachter still have a branch office here? This one looked exactly like those I remembered; but the driver crossed himself as he smilingly signalled to me to proceed, and on closer inspection I saw what had happened. It was simply the 'Swastika Laundry', which had painted the year of its founding, 1912, clearly beneath the swastika; but the mere possibility that it might have been one of those others was enough to take my breath away.

The vans used by the Swastika Laundry didn't operate on diesel or petrol; they were electric, far ahead of their time.

The Spring Grove Laundry bought the company out in 1987, and sold the land for redevelopment in the early 2000s. The only reminder of the Swastika Laundry at the site today, now known as The Oval, is the huge chimney, now a protected structure, which was emblazoned with a huge swastika until the late 1980s.

59.

Original pirate material

While much has been written of Ireland's 'Super Pirate' radio stations like Radio Nova and Sunshine Radio, and some stations like Phantom have made the great leap to respectability, there is a whole hidden history to Irish pirate radio that has gone largely unexplored. The earliest pirate radio stations in Ireland were schoolboy efforts that the state wished to suppress quickly, and that in some ways were ahead of official broadcasting.

Over the Christmas holidays in 1967, a group of schoolboys began transmitting music and stories across the airwaves, attracting the attention of the national media. An *Irish Times* report on the schoolboy station noted that from 'somewhere south of the Liffey' these young boys had made two one-hour broadcasts, at 8 a.m. and 12.30 p.m., on 22 December. The paper noted that 'pop music programmes were interspersed with greetings from the announcer to school friends. The transmissions also featured excerpts from satirical magazine, *Private Eye*'. In the playful spirit of the station, listeners who tuned in at 1.30 p.m. were told by a young boy in fits of giggles that they had come to the wrong place if they wanted to hear the news, and that they should perhaps turn over to Radió Éireann. This was Radio Jacqueline.

This all sounds harmless enough of course, but the Department of Posts and Telegraphs found little funny about Radio Jacqueline, with the department telling the newspapers that the youngsters would be tracked down, and that these pirate broadcasts could interfere with legitimate radio transmissions.

This was not the first schoolboy attempt at radio production in 1960s Ireland. Three years earlier, in Cork, Radio Juliet had been born. This was a station operated by a dozen students with a wide variety of content. The *Irish Independent* noted that the station played pop music in the morning and classical works in the afternoon. It also contained newscasts with local, national and even international focus, not to mention weather reports. The station was operated on a rather modest budget of £1 a day, and news reports noted the boys would use Shakespearean names to contact one another, owing to Radió Éireann authorities being in pursuit! Remarkably, the boys themselves had constructed the station's transmitter at a cost of £6. The station lasted just a number of days before it was suppressed, with the Department of Posts and Telegraphs refusing a request for an interview from the teenage directors or Radio Juliet.

An *Irish Times* journalist would report that Radio Juliet was the first 'non-political pirate radio station' in the state. But following the suppression of Radio Juliet, the man behind what was in fact the state's first pirate station was about to come forward in the letters pages of a national broadsheet.

In a fascinating letter, written to the *Irish Independent*, Jim O' Carroll of Limerick noted that he himself had constructed a transmitter in 1934, and that this effort became known locally in Limerick as 'the Pirate Radio'. O' Carroll noted that in his view 'we have exactly the same system governing broadcasting as Communist Russia – one programme, one official voice'.

O' Carroll also thankfully wrote his memories of this 1934 station for the *Old Limerick Journal*, noting that he called himself Billy Dynamite on air, with his friend Charlie O'Connor joining him and adopting the name Al Dubbin. These youngsters operated their station under the title City Broadcasting Service, or CBS for short, and tended to broadcast between 7 p.m. and 11 p.m. O' Carroll recalled that 'providing four hours of entertainment every night was difficult, to say the least, considering that Radió Éireann, with all the resources of the state, was providing a mere five'.

Every evening, young Charlie would cycle to the railway station to collect the Dublin evening papers, which O' Carroll would then read on air. The suppression of this station made the front page of the *Irish Press* newspaper, which ran with the headline 'Pirate Caught – Transmitter Seized!'

In time, pirate radio stations would develop into something much more advanced than some of the ventures discussed here. By the late 1970s and into the 1980s, pirate stations enjoyed huge popularity among Irish youth, offering something different from the state radio service, with even the political establishment availing of the reach of these stations for paid advertisements. Things had come a long way from Jim O' Carroll's 1934 experiment!

60.

May your love shine a light

Walking up the North Circular Road, it's impossible not to be taken in by the sight of the historic floodlights of Dalymount Park. Part of Dublin's skyline for over 50 years, they stand like dinosaurs from another age, beacons calling the League of Ireland faithful to Phibsboro on match nights. These kinds of pylons are a rare, dying breed proper to stadiums in the lower echelons of football, and reminders of its urban, working-class roots. Nestled behind rows of Victorian houses and Phibsboro Shopping centre, finding Dalymount without them would be a struggle.

The floodlights were installed in early 1962 and had come second hand from Arsenal's Highbury Stadium at a cost of €18,000. They oversaw their first competitive game between a Bohemian XI select and a visiting Arsenal side on Wednesday 7 March of that year; the away side coming out with a convincing 8-3 victory. The installation of the floodlights was Bohemians' side of a gentleman's agreement with the FAI, who in

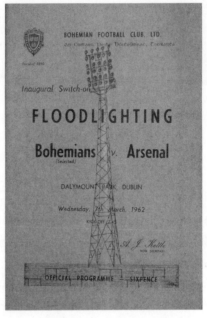

Programme from the inaugural floodlit game at Dalymount
Park. (Mick Morgan)

return would host all major soccer internationals in
Dalymount.

Only a couple of years into the agreement, however,
the FAI moved the games to Lansdowne Road, where
they remain to this day.

The huge outlay at that time, and lack of return on
investment, caused Bohemians to struggle financially
for the rest of the sixties, forcing their hand somewhat
in the latter years of the decade when amateur players
left in their droves for paid employment, and the

club were forced to turn semi-professional in order to survive. Bohemians went on to win two league titles, two FAI Cups and two league cups in the 1970s, and fifty years after their installation, the phrase 'just follow the floodlights' is still used when directing visitors to Dalymount Park.

61.

A conversation with Philip Chevron

2012 marks the 35th anniversary of Dublin punks The Radiators from Space's first single 'Television Screen'.

It'll also see the release of their fourth studio album, *Sound City Beat*. As such, I thought that there would be no better time to sit down and have a chat with lead singer and songwriter Philip Chevron; in my opinion, one of the greatest songwriters ever to come out of our fair city. (The full interview can be read on the blog).

So, were your parents from Dublin?

Yep, both inner-city kids. My mother was from the Liberties, hence the Huguenot connection. A lot of them ended up in the Liberties … as artisans and tradesman. My dad was from Ballybough. So basically they were north and south inner city. Absolutely dye-din-the-wool Dublin, going back several generations. My father's mother was from Drogheda. That's the only Culchie blood at all … and that only counts as north Dublin now anyways!

In my mother's case, her father was a trader in Dublin Corporation Fruit Market. He traded in potatoes … and supplied Tayto crisps. It was one of the big contracts you could get at the time. That elevated my grandfather into the frontline of the new middle classes in Dublin. As soon as they could, they got the hell out of the Liberties and moved to Terenure. My mother was still a Liberties girl at heart though. She loved the fact that she moved up in the world.

My father stayed in Ballybough all along. There is that strange reverse snobbishness in Dublin as well, where my mother would say, 'We live in Terenure, but we're from the Liberties!'

I heard your father's mother was politically active?

Yes, She was in Cumann na mBan … but I found out after she died that her view of it was that it was great way to meet fellas. There was a bit of craic involved in it, hiding the guns in the prams. Innocence that only a 17-year-old girl could have really. That's probably why they got away with it. Like everybody, she hated the Black and Tans and wanted to see the back of them, but more than anything it was 'I wonder will your man be at the dance on Saturday night?'

My grandfather on my mother's side, the potato merchant, was one of those Dubliners who covered all angles. He was in the Knights of Columbanus, in the old IRA I think but also the Masons. People then were pragmatic. They weren't dogmatic or ideologists; idealists maybe though. They did what they had to do. If you're a tradesman in Dublin, you had to keep everyone happy. Strangely, at his funeral in the early 1960s, he had 15-gun salute from the IRA. I was like 'what the fuck?' Nobody knew. People thought 'well then, I guess he must have been in the IRA'. I thought, well, 'they don't take the guns out for the fun of it'.

The Civil War caused such a rift in this country. It's as solid, in its own way, as the one that still separates America. In a sense, the Irish were incapable of talking about it. I suppose we all went through our lives not talking about it. Truth is, we will never know if there were 25,000 people in the GPO in 1916.

Do you think the Civil War wounds are finally healing now? Is this the first generation that we can see that?

I wonder about that. Maybe the de Valera generation *is* dead. I don't know. They might go away for a few years but they'll be back. Hopefully, it is a generation thing. I know one of my uncles still praises Bertie after all this time. It's because these family bonds die very hard. Saying that, I don't know anyone personally under 70 who thinks like that. I think we've got through the worst of it. We've had a century of bullshit from the politicians, priests, teachers and everyone else as well.

I genuinely believe that people are moving forward. It feels like people aren't so easily prepared to take the bullshit, on face value anyway. The whole generation that came up during the time of The Radiators, not just musically but in literature, art, film and theatre, were the first to have had the courage, or the space maybe, to say, 'Let's change it! It's crap!'

It was kind of tentative because we all felt we were kind of transgressing in some deeply important way. In that, we were almost being anti-Irish, anti-Catholic and anti-everything.

The generation, who are now in their early 50s to early 60s, all felt individually that we were the only ones who felt this way. But when you got to meet people at The Project Arts Centre, you realised that other people were speaking the same language as you. In some ways, Geldof knocked down the last wall by saying 'I'm going to talk about this – whether you like it or not'. Had we be been more aware that there was this greater movement towards change; it probably would have been a lot louder and angrier.

But we also had a thing when just on the cusp of change it was 'one step forward, two steps back'. Look at the reaction to the Pope visit in 1979. I remember thinking 'hang on, things aren't going the right way'. Suddenly there was a whole generation being named John Paul. It was strange.

Would it be fair to say that you were trying to deal with the topic of Irish nationalism in your second album Ghostown? *Specifically 'They're Looting in the Town'?*

Like a number of the songs from that album, they appear to go in one direction and then they divert completely, which was deliberate.

I loved *Ulysses* but I never got through the whole thing. I loved the idea of it. 'Kitty Ricketts' is directly out of it. I loved *Strumpet City* because it was the first novel that manifested, in an interesting way, the people who were involved in the 1913 Lockout and how people responded to the Rising.

The Jim Larkin statue was probably a catalyst. It was unveiled in '77 I think. It was the first 'real' person we had in that street. O'Connell and Parnell were all in the 'pre-history'. The Jim Larkin statue chimed with Strumpet history.

I remember thinking that these people were fucking pagans! They liked to drink, shag and went to mass if they had to. Essentially, they were a socialistic people who wanted their country back, but not in a violent way if at all possible. James Plunkett was the first to animate it in a literary way. I felt that this was a country that had long been under the thumb of not just the British Empire but also the forces of the Vatican, pretty much equally. Shane feels the same way, incidentally. There's a real, living, breathing culture of actual people who feel things and think about things in a certain way underneath these ciphers of twentieth-century Ireland made up of paupers, patriots and priests.

Back to 'They're Looting in the Town', the Lockout started off that song. Irish citizens being slaughtered for being involved in a trade union. In the 1960s and 1970s, the tenants of Sean O'Casey plays were still living in the same slums. Somehow, people had been left out of this social bargain. We talk today about the 99% and the 1% – it's not that different at all.

62.

The forgotten Captain Ingram

Captain James Robert Ingram, the first Chief Officer of the Dublin Fire Brigade, is today buried in an unmarked grave in Mount Jerome Cemetery. Ingram, who modelled the first Dublin Fire Brigade on that of New York City, died not fighting the flames of Dublin but rather due to tuberculosis.

Dublin has had provisions for fighting fires since the late sixteenth century, indeed Parish churches were required to keep buckets and ladders in an ordinance of 1592, but the city itself purchased its first fire engines in 1711. In 2011, the 300th anniversary of this event passed the city by without being marked in any way. Saint Werburgh's Church on Werburgh Street boasts the oldest surviving fire appliances in the city. Such appliances are said to be the origin of the term 'parish pump', a term more often heard in Irish political life than fire fighting today.

In 1862, Dublin got a municipal fire service, established following a series of serious fires in the city, including one at the Kildare Street Club in November of

1860, which cost three lives and destroyed the home from home of the Anglo Irish ascendency. The contemporary fire service of the city dates back to 1862, established by an Act of Parliament. In its search for a man to lead this new service, the Dublin Corporation turned to Robert Ingram, a Dubliner who had learned the trade on the streets of New York, despite having been born in the Irish capital in 1830. Ingram emigrated to New York in 1851, first earning a living as a banknote engraver, before joining the Niagra Hose Company in Lower Manhattan, one of the many colourful volunteer fire companies which made up the New York Fire Department. His experience in the United States made him the perfect candidate in the eyes of the Dublin Corporation.

With Ingram's appointment, the 'Dublin Fire Department', as it was initially known, was born. Ingram recruited 40 men, many of them previously sailors, and, perhaps in tribute to his former colleagues in the New York Fire Department, Dublin's earliest fire-fighters wore a uniform of red flannel shirts. The officers of this new service wore a uniform that was a copy of the frock coat and kepi of a United States Army officer.

Ingram's headquarters was established at South William Street, in the premises that in later years would become the Municipal Museum. This important historic site of Dublin's first fire station is unmarked today, with no plaque upon it informing Dublin of what once stood opposite the location of the Pygmalion bar and club today. There was also a substation at Winetavern Street, on the site of what is today the Civic Offices.

Ingram's small band of fire-fighters found themselves up against many different threats in Victorian Dublin. The tenements, mills and factories of Dublin all presented their own dangers. The Corporation decorated many of these early fire-fighters for their efforts. At times, Ingram would find himself having to resort to most unusual methods. On one occasion, Ingram stemmed the flow of burning spirits from a distillery in the Liberties by loading horse manure onto the streets, and on another occasion he dealt with a ship drifting into Dublin Port ablaze by ordering the Royal Navy to open fire on it and sink it into the bay.

This heroic public servant, a remarkable character, died in May 1882, 20 years after his return to his home city to found what we now know as Dublin Fire Brigade. He died at the young age of 52. For a man who had fought the flames of New York and then Dublin, it was tragic that tuberculosis would claim his life. This shocking fact has now become clear through a report from Captain Thomas Purcell, a later head of the Dublin Fire Brigade who, in 1892, would compile a list detailing the cause of death for members of the brigade during the previous decade. The nature of Ingram's job brought him into the tenements of Dublin, where tuberculosis was rife among the working class and impoverished of the city.

The Dublin Fire Brigade is now over 150 years in existence, yet the final resting spot of the man who started it all remains unmarked.

63.

When Bovril lit up College Green

The neon Bovril advertisement sign that once stood high above the James Fox Cigar and Whiskey Store building at the corner of Grafton Street and College Green is fondly remembered by a generation of Dubliners. Stories abound of how young kids, city visitors and tipplers after a night out often went out of their way to head down by Trinity to view this extraordinary wonder. The sign was unique at the time, as each of its letters could light up in a different colour.

The original Bovril sign was the first illuminated advertisement of its kind in Dublin. It was erected around 1909, and remained there for over 30 years.

In September 1920, Messrs Bovril agreed to temporarily shut down their sign because of coal shortages. It was noted in 1930 that the annual cost of maintaining the sign was £50. While expensive for the time, Bovril said that 'the signs are seen by thousands of people every night of the year', and as such can be seen as an 'extremely cheap' advertising medium.

In August 1939, Bovril replaced the old sign with a 'handsome Sunray Electric Sign'.

James Punkett, author of *Strumpet City*, called it a 'great wonder', and wrote in 1991 that as a child:

> The Bovril sign … would put its breathtaking fireworks display against the night sky and command my enchanted attention.

Samuel Beckett's collection of short prose *More Pricks Than Kicks* (1934) depicts protagonist Belacqua Shuah's perception of the misty neon streetscape of College Green outside of Trinity College Dublin:

> Bright and cheery above the storm of the Green, as though coached by the Star of Bethlehem, the Bovril sign danced and danced through its seven phases.

Quidnunc in *The Irish Times* in 1939 wrote:

> For years it has twinkled green to white to red in all their combinations. It caught the eye of all coming down Westmoreland Street, and it is not so very long ago that people used to stand and watch its changes, so few were illuminated signs in the city.

The TCD Miscellany made the following humorous observation in a short poem entitled 'Epitaph' in 1951:

Here Lies one who met his fate
Just outside the College Gate;
By darkness saw he sights superb,
With eyes aloft he left the kerb;
As from beneath the 'bus they picked him
They murmured 'Boveril's latest victim'

Éamonn Mac Thomáis in his classic memoir *Me jewel and darlin' Dublin* (1983) wrote:

The first illuminated sign I remember seeing in Dublin was the Bovril sign high over College Green. What a spectacle it provided as it burst into a rainbow of colours.

A simpler time, certainly.

64.

The tragic death of Kathleen Wright, Trinity College Dublin

One of the more unusual pieces of propaganda ever issued by Irish republicans is undoubtedly *The Good Old IRA: Tan War Operations*, a 1985 text issued by the 'Publicity Department' of Sinn Féin. It was an attempt by Irish republicans in the 1980s to highlight how they felt those in the media and authority romanticised the actions of republicans in the early twentieth century, while vilifying contemporary republicans. It is a shocking read, with over 60 pages detailing atrocities committed during the revolutionary period by Irish republicans.

The work's introduction slates Labour Party leader and 'Free State deputy-premier' Dick Spring, for example, noting that he was:

> ...tongue-tied in attempting to explain the differences between the IRA gunrunner Roger Casement [in whose honour he was unveiling a statue at Ballyheigue, County Kerry] and those IRA gunrunners on the Marita Ann who had

been arrested by his government's forces off the Kerry coast 24 hours previously.

One incident detailed in particular, from 1921, stood out for me. It is listed on page 56 of the work, under the title 'Not Cricket', and describes the killing of a civilian spectator at a cricket match by republicans in June 1921:

> One woman spectator, Miss Kate Wright, a student of Trinity College, was killed and another wounded in an attack by armed civilians on military officers playing in a cricket match at Trinity College Dublin on June 3rd. A man fired shots onto the field of play from the railings at Nassau Street from which the pitch was visible.

The Irish Times reported on the day following the shooting that:

> The occasion was one of festivity and enjoyment in the College Park. A cricket match in connection with Warriors' Day was in progress. The teams were the Gentlemen of Ireland versus the Military of Ireland. The general belief is that the latter were the objects of the murderous attack which resulted so tragically.

From the contemporary newspaper reports, we can establish quite a lot about Miss Wright. Aged only 21 (based on an *Irish Independent* report of the inquiry into her death), Kathleen Alexanderson Wright was engaged to be married to a young man who was also a student at the Dublin University. His name was Mr George Herbert Ardall, and he was a native of Sligo. He was studying Science at the University, and was with Kathleen enjoying the cricket match, on what was said to be a lovely summer's day in Dublin.

Kathleen was the daughter of the Reverend E.A. Wright of All Saints Clapham Park in London, and the *Irish Independent* of June 4 1921 noted that he had 'before going to England filled curacies in Cahir and Seapatrick', both in County Down. At the time of the shooting she was living on Pembroke Road in Rathmines, but beforehand had lived in digs at Trinity.

The *Irish Independent* reported how he told the inquiry into his fiancée's death that:

> When the shots were fired he pulled Miss Wright down on the ground as quickly as he could. She was moaning, but he was not certain she was hit until a few moments afterwards when he saw blood on the front of her blouse. Three doctors attended her, and one told him that the case was absolutely hopeless. He did not hear her make any remark. He accompanied her to hospital, where he was told she was dead.

The Irish Times report into the inquiry noted that:

Another witness stated that he was in the cricket pavilion, and heard someone remark that shots were being fired outside in the park. He went out immediately, and ran to where a crowd was collecting inside the park railings opposite the Kildare Street Club. A few of his friends told him what had happened and said that the shots came through the railings [...] When witnesses arrived at where the girl was lying on the ground the crowd who are usually gathered in Nassau Street outside the railings to watch the game had all cleared off.

Perhaps the most surreal details about the shooting come from the statement issued by Dublin Castle in the immediate aftermath of the event. The official report noted that another female was wounded during the shootings, and provided great insight into the initial reaction of those on the green:

As soon as the shooting began, the players, realising what was happening, threw themselves flat on the field. A regimental band, which was on the field at the time, threw down their instruments and also lay prone. The spectators were not so quick to realise what was happening until a number of shots had been fired and persons were hit.

The attackers made good their escape. While nobody was ever tried for the shooting of Miss Kathleen Wright, and little was written about her after her body returned home, the identities of the republicans responsible has come to light. In *Sleep Soldier Sleep: The Life and Times of Padraig O'Connor,* it is noted that an Active Service Unit of the IRA in Dublin 'received instructions to disrupt a cricket match between the "Gentlemen of Ireland" and a team of British military officers in Trinity College'. Paddy O'Connor and Jimmy McGuinness took up position behind the Trinity boundary wall at Lincoln Place and fired upon the match. It is stated that Paddy O'Connor later expressed deep regret at the killing of young Kathleen, which proved a propaganda disaster for republicans. According to an account written years later for the *Dublin Brigade Review:*

> A Miss Alexander Wright (a spectator) becoming frightened started into the line of fire of one of the snipers and was killed. The accident was very much regretted by the man concerned.

Padraig O'Connor would later go on to fight on the Pro-Treaty side in the Civil War, and was involved in the execution of figures such as Erskine Childers. Years later, he would tell Ernie O'Malley, a prominent opponent of the Anglo-Irish Treaty, that 'the executions broke your morale, there is no doubt about that. The executions were deliberately used as a means to break your resistance'.

65.

Little John & Dublin

There is an enduring but surprisingly little researched local legend that suggests that Little John of Robin Hood fame visited Dublin in the twelfth century.

The first reference I could find comes from Richard Stanihurst, who wrote in in 1577 that:

> In the yeere one thousand one hundred foure score and nine ... little John was faine to flee the realme by sailing into Ireland, where he sojorned for a few daies in Dublin. The citizens being done to understand the wandering outcast to be an excellent archer, requestd him hartilie to trie how far he could at randon; who yeelding to their behest, stood on the bridge of Dublin, and shot at the mole hill, leving behind him a monument, rather by his posteritie to be woondered than possiblie by anie man living to be counter-scored.

Joseph Cooper's Walker's *Historical Memories of the Irish Bards* (1786) fleshes out the story:

According to tradition, Little John (who followed his master to this country) shot an arrow from the old bridge to the present site of St. Michan's Church, a distance of about 11 score and seven yards, but poor Little John's great practical skill in archery could not save him from an ignominious fate; as it appears from the records of the Southwell family, he was publicly executed for robbery on Arbour Hill.

The 'old bridge' mentioned is the Father Mathew Bridge, which has been there in one shape or another for over 1,000 years. A very interesting article on the history of this bridge by Frank Hopkins also mentions the Little John legend, claiming that it was from Father Mathew Bridge that 'Little John allegedly shot an arrow all the way to Oxmanstown.'

The *Dublin University Magazine* (1857) suggests that:

… after the dissolution of the band in Sherwood forest … (Little John) while jouring for a few days in Dublin exhibited to the citizens by shooting an arrow from the Old Bridge to a distant hillock on the northern side of the city, thence styled in after time 'Little John's shot'.

The historical memoirs of the city of Armagh (1819) also mentions in passing that 'Little John … had visited

Dublin about the year 1188 and had shot an arrow from Dublin Bridge to the little hill in Oxmantown'.

The wonderfully named Pat Chat wrote in *The Irish Times* in 1882 that 'Little John ... exhibited feats of archery ... [but] was then hanged at Arbour Hill for robbery'.

D.H.W., in his article entitled 'Little John in Ireland: An Exile from Sherwood' (1928) proposes that Little John and his followers 'lived in the woods outside Dublin, round Arbour Hill', and reiterated the tale that 'he was caught in Dublin ... [and] was publicly executed on Arbour Hill'.

Like most stories about Robin Hood, there is little that can be backed up by historical evidence. For example, Little John is reputed to be buried in a churchyard in the village of Hathersage, Derbyshire. A modern tombstone marks the supposed location of his grave, which lies under an old yew tree.

However, I much prefer the version that he was hanged at Arbour Hill and is buried a few feet below James Connolly.

66.

A historic junction at Pearse Street

For nearly 1,200 years there has been a sculpture at the junction of College Street with Pearse Street and D'Olier Street. Firstly, the Long Stone (c.837–c.1700), then the Crampton Memorial (1862–1959) and finally the Long Stone replica (1986–present). The old Viking 'Long Stone', a 12ft to 14ft megalith, was first constructed by Norsemen in 837AD to symbolise their possession of the surrounding lands. Historian George Thomas Stokes summed it up well when said that the historic stone 'escaped all the vicissitudes of time, the invasions of the Danes, the wars of Celts and Saxons, the struggles of Royalists and Republicans'.

John W. De Courcy, in his 1996 book on the Liffey, described the history of the Long Stone. The procession riding the city franchises in 1488 passed 'by the long stone of the Stayn', and in 1625 the road from the city to Lazar's Hill was known as 'the lane leading to Long Stone'. In 1607, the pillar was being used as a mark in the work of land surveyors, and Petty in 1654 shows its location inside the shoreline. Within ten years of Petty's map, Hawkins's Wall (1662–3) would place 150m of dry ground between the Long Stone and the new hightide shoreline. It would then become known as the 'longe stone over against the College'. It continued to be used as a land surveyor's mark until at least 1679.

The stone disappeared from public view during the latter part of the seventeenth century, when William Davis, the City Recorder, was improving his property

Long Stone replica, erected 1986. Designed by Cliodhna Cussen. Situated on the site of the original Viking Long Stone, which was there for over 850 years. (Paul Reynolds)

near Saint Andrew's Church. During this time, the Long Stone was either removed or stolen, and was last seen lying against a fence in the grounds of Trinity College according to Frank Hopkins. However, De Courcy suggests that it could be 'be buried in the area and still intact.'

The Crampton Memorial, known colloquially as 'the Water Baby' and 'the Cauliflower', took its place and was situated at the junction of College Street with Pearse Street and D'Olier Street for nearly 100 years. It was designed by John Robinson Kirk and was named after Sir Philip Crampton (1777–1858), an eminent surgeon and anatomist. The memorial, which was made up of a stone base with three drinking fountains, slowly fell apart and was finally removed in 1959.

In 1986, a replica of the Long Stone was erected. It was designed by Cliodhna Cussen, mother of Sinn Fein TD Aengus Ó Snodaigh and Rossa, Rónán, and Colm of trad band Kíla. The 11-foot granite sculpture has the head of Ivar, the first Norse King of Dublin, who is believed to have erected the original Stein on the base of one side and a head of a nun from the Priory of All Hallows, which is thought to have been situated on the site in the Middle Ages, on the other.

One wonders whether it will last as long as the original.

67.

Dominic Behan, out of the shadow

On Kildare Road in Kimmage, a small plaque above the door of number 70 tells passers-by that it is a building of historical importance. The plaque shows the face of Brendan Behan, alongside the years of his birth and passing. Behan was a giant of Irish literature of course, but 70 Kildare Road was a home in which the sound of music and the typewritten word emerged from all rooms. The children of Stephen and Kathleen Behan would all reflect the rich literary interests and passions of their parents, and the contribution of Brendan's younger brother Dominic to the worlds of stage, song and literature cannot be overstated. A committed socialist and republican, Dominic would publish his first poems and prose in the pages of the magazine of Na Fianna Éireann, and in time would become a writer celebrated by voices as diverse as John Lennon and James Plunkett.

The Behan boys were products of the inner city, to whom Russell Street was home. Stephen Behan, the father, was a veteran of the War of Independence, and the Civil War that followed. At the time that Brendan was born

Illustration of Dominic Behan (Luke Fallon)

in 1923, Stephen was imprisoned in Kilmainham Gaol. Dominic was born in October of 1928, into a different environment from that of the Civil War backdrop, and at a time that he joked saw the:

National movement in the hands of priests and politicians who had never fired a shot in anger, except during the grouse season, a new nation was planned, for the benefit of Irish-Irelander businessmen and shopkeepers.

Kathleen, wife of Stephen, was an equally remarkable influence on the children, educating them in a way that would shape their politics and literary passions. Kathleen would take the children on walks through the city, and as Ulick O'Connor noted in his biography of Brendan, she would show them not only the places where the city's revolutionaries were born or executed, but the houses of Shaw, Swift and Wilde too.

Dominic remembered Russell Street fondly, and recalled that 'the native industries of Russell Street were drink and cleanliness, represented respectively by the Mountjoy Brewery and the Phoenix Laundry.' With a greengrocers, bookmakers and pub, Dominic joked in his memoirs *Teems of Times and Happy Returns* that there thus existed no reason for anyone to leave the confines of the street, unless off to work.

The 1930s would see so many inner-city Dublin families like the Behans moved to the new, emerging suburbs, and thus Kildare Road would become home to the family in 1937. To the boys, suburbia was jokingly known as 'Siberia', with their new home as far removed from the life and character of Russell Street as was possible. Dominic would recall his brother Brendan joking that:

They could've built flats in the centre of the town for us and kept reservations like this for them that come in from the country. Home from home it would have been. But us! And the only grass we ever saw we were asked to keep off it.

Republicanism was at the heart of the Behan's very being, and as a youngster Dominic would join Na Fianna Éireann. When Brendan was arrested in 1939, Dominic would recall that 'he delivered a highly romantic speech in which he defended the ideal of an Irish Workers' and Small Farmers' Republic'. Stephen Behan was considered among the best sign painters in Dublin, and worked as a contractor. Brendan and Dominic worked on several sites together in the 1940s following Brendan's release. One foreman complained to Stephen about the two brothers, stating that they were 'the greatest bastards I've ever come across. One wants the men to strike for an incentive bonus so that the other one can bring them down to the pub to drink it.'

Dominic's politics were motivated first and foremost by a class consciousness, which would see him in trouble on several occasions in the early 1950s for his role in protests against the unemployment crisis of the period, and indeed he was jailed for his activism. Dominic married Josephine Quinn upon his release from prison, and it should be noted that Quinn also came from a family of strong left-wing stock, who had a history of activism with the Communist Party in Glasgow. They would emigrate to London, yet the late 1950s would bring considerable success for Dominic in Dublin.

Dominic's first play, *Posterity be Damned*, was first performed in the Gaiety in September 1959. Set between a council house and the cellar of a pub, Dominic remarked to journalists at the time that the play attempted to deal 'with the recurrent appeal of an illegal army to successive generations of young Irishmen'. The part of the ballad singer who links the story together on stage was played by Dominic himself, and the play received fantastic reviews. When asked by a reporter when he himself would produce a play, owing to the successes of his sons, Stephen Behan responded by asking 'why should I produce plays when I produce playwrights?' Dominic noted as he spoke before the crowd after the play's first performance that it was his first time speaking in public in Dublin since taking the platform at a demonstration of the unemployed. Other acclaimed plays would follow, including *The Folk Singer* in 1972, dealing with the situation in Ulster at the time.

In addition to the success of Behan's stage work, he would achieve fantastic reviews as a writer. *Teems of Times and Happy Returns*, Behan's autobiographical novel, was first published in England in 1961. Its first edition was banned in

Ireland, and the first Irish edition did not follow until 1979, from Repsol Press. Dominic dedicated that edition to Irish republicans Malachy McGurran and Billy McMillen, who were both killed in the 1970s. Three years on from *Teems and Times*, a half-hour programme Dominic produced for Telefís Éireann proved so popular that it attracted the attention of

Billboard magazine in the United States, who noted that many were calling for more from Dominic. Dominic's contribution to the television screen was not restricted to Ireland, and his *A Better Class of Folk*, produced for Scottish Television, was also greatly praised.

Dominic was not alone a fine singer, but a songwriter of great ability. While songs like 'McAlpine's Fusiliers' and 'The Patriot Game' are widely known and sung today, it is often forgotten that they were written by Dominic.

Dominic passed away in 1989, far from an old man at 60. His ashes were scattered on the waters of the Royal Canal, near his beloved Russell Street, and the then General Secretary of the Workers' Party Seán Garland officiated at the ceremony, delivering an oration in his honour.

He was remembered in the pages of *The Irish Times* as 'a funny man, garrulous, brilliant, infuriating, angry, lovable but never boring' by P. McG., who recalled once finding a crumpled note from Dominic on which he had written 'I, Dominic Behan, do hereby declare that I am a true Republican in the tradition of Wolfe Tone and any man who says otherwise slanders me.'

68.

The Oak Bar & Crane Lane

The Oak Bar, established in 1860 at the corner of Dame Street and Crane Lane, boasts a fascinating history, as its interior was built with the remnants of an old ship.

The Dublin Street Directory of 1862 shows that the occupant of 81 Dame Street was a P.J. Burke, a grocer and home & foreign spirit dealer. In the early 1920s, the bar was bought by the Humphrys family. To this day, you can still see the original tiled floor sign at the entrance reminding customers of its former name.

After a redecoration in 1946, the name of the pub was changed to The Oak. Why was this? The oak-panelled interior of the bar was made with wood salvaged from the RMS *Mauretania*, the sister ship of the RMS *Lusitania*.

The RMS *Mauretania* was launched in 1906, and at the time was the largest and fastest ship in the world. During the First World War, it served as a troopship to carry British troops during the Gallipoli campaign. The ship was withdrawn from service in 1934 and its furnishings and fittings were put up for auction.

Crane Lane, the little street at the side of The Oak that connects Dame Street with East Essex Street, is also historic in its own right. This narrow thoroughfare, which is now most famous for housing The Boilerhouse gay sauna, was once the primary route to Dublin Castle before Parliament Street was constructed. It takes its name from a public crane used to unload ships that was erected nearby in 1571 beside the old Custom House, the site of the Clarence Hotel today. A previous crane had been put in place here by the Normans in the thirteenth century.

Ireland's first synagogue was founded in Crane Lane by Portuguese Jews. It was in existence from at least 1700, though some historians such as Pat Liddy believe it dates back to the 1660s. The prayer rooms were said to have been in the house of a merchant called Phillips. Unfortunately, it is not known in which building on Crane Lane Phillips resided.

During the 1700s, a drinking spot called the The Bear Tavern stood in Crane Lane. In the later half of the eighteenth century, another 'more frequented' tavern, according to Sir John Thomas Gilbert , was run there by a Freemason named David Cobert, an 'excellent musician' and leader of the band of the Dublin Independent Volunteers. Around the same time, the *Dublin Gazette* was printed in the Custom-House Printing-House in Crane Lane by Edward Sandys.

While the history of Dublin's main streets are usually well documented, it is the narrow little alleys like Crane Lane that are often overlooked.

69.

Prince Albert on College Green

On 27 February 1864, *The Nation* newspaper reported on a 'ingrate and dishonouring act' carried out by Dublin Corporation, when the Corporation decided upon Prince Albert, and not Henry Grattan, for the prime statue location at College Green. The paper ran a selection of extracts from other papers across the island, which all slammed the decision, with the Wexford People noting that 'thirty-two against fourteen decided that Henry Grattan might go seek a place elsewhere, and that Prince Albert should be the choice of Ireland.' By December 1865, *The Nation* was boasting that the planned 'German invasion' of College Green, in the form of a statue of Prince Albert, was no more. There had been protests against the statue, for example a meeting at the Rotunda that saw Fenians take the stage. The Lord Mayor had read a letter from the Duke of Leinster in Council that proposed that the Prince Albert Statue Committee erect their monument to Albert in the grounds of the Royal Dublin Society House. 'The idea that Prince Albert's statue would ever be raised in College Green was manifestly as hopeless and wild as a design to move the Hill of Howth', the paper stated, and the planned 'desecration' of College Green, an area historically associated with Henry Grattan and his Irish Volunteers, had been averted. 'The husband of the famine Queen' was not to have pride of place on College Green.

College Green would become home to John Henry Foley's statue of Grattan, a statue unveiled on 6 January 1875. At that unveiling, A.M. Sullivan spoke of how:

> … this is an age where in other lands principles are abroad teaching class to war upon class. Come hither, Irish men … behold the figure of a man who, born in the highest sphere of society, had a heart that felt for the poorest cottager on an Irish hillside.

The Irish Times report on the unveiling of the statue noted that the position was perfect for a monument to Grattan, alongside Parliament and facing his alma mater. 'His statue has been placed on the only site in Ireland that was worthy of the man, fronting equally two buildings with which his name will be forever most gloriously associated.'

Today, Prince Albert can be found in the back of Leinster House, beside the railings of the Natural History Museum. It is a far cry from College Green, and he is certainly a forgotten imperial monument.

Select Bibliography

Newspapers:
An Phoblacht
Freemans Journal
Irish Independent
Irish Press
Leitrim Observer
Republican Congress
Sunday Independent
The Irish Times
The Nation
The Times (London)
The Worker
The Workers' Republic

Magazines and Journals:
An tÓglách
Dublin Historical Record
Dublin Opinion
Dublin Penny Journal
History Ireland
Hot Press
Look Left Magazine
Old Limerick Journal

Saothar
Studies
The Bell
The Dubliner
The Irish Monthly
Time Magazine

Online Resources:

Arthur Lloyd Music Hall and Theatre History site at
http://www.arthurlloyd.co.uk

Bureau of Military History at http://www.bureauofmil-
itaryhistory.ie/

Cork Multitext Project (UCC) at http://multitext.ucc.ie/

Dictionary of Irish Biography. http://dib.campbridge.
org

Dublin.ie http://www.dublin.ie

Humphry family website. http://www.humphrysfami-
lytree.com

Irish Medals website at http://www.irishmedals.org

Me Jewel and Darlin' Dublin http://www.mejeweland-
darlin.com

National Library of Ireland archive at http://www.nli.ie
Storymap at http://www.storymap.ie

Archival Sources:

Department of Justice Files at National Archives,
Bishop Street.

Dublin Corporation Minute Books at Dublin City
Archive, Pearse Street.

Print Sources:

Bateson, Ray. *They Died by Pearse's Side*. Dublin, 2010.

Behan, Dominic. *Teems of Times and Happy Returns*. London,1961.

Blackwood, William. *Blackwood's Edinburgh Magazine, Volume 9*. London, 1821.

Böll, Heinrich. *Irisches Tagebuch*. Colonge, 1961.

Collins, Lorcan. *James Connolly*. Dublin, 2012.

Crowe, Catriona (ed). *Dublin 1911*. Dublin, 2011.

De Courcy, John W. *The Liffey in Dublin*. Dublin, 1996.

Dixon, Stephen and Deirdre Falvey. *Gift of the Gag: The Explosion in Irish Comedy*. Belfast, 1999.+

Doyle, Bob. *Brigadista*. Dublin, 2006.

Doughlas, R.M *Architects of the Resurrection: Ailtirí na hAiséirghe and the fascist 'new order' in Ireland* . Manchester, 2009.

Fagan, Terry. *Monto: Madams, Murder and Black Coddle*. Dublin, 2000.

Fallon, Las. *Dublin Fire Brigade and the Irish Revolution*. Dublin, 2012.

Ferriter, Diarmaid. *The Transformation of Ireland: 1900–2000*. London, 2004.

Forde, Frank. *The long watch: the history of the Irish mercantile marine in World War Two*. Dublin, 1981.

Greaves, C. Desmond. *Liam Mellowes and the Irish Revolution*. Belfast, 1971.

Greaves, C.Desmond. *The Irish Transport and General Workers' Union: The Formative Years, 1900–23*. Dublin,1982.

Hanley, Brian. *The IRA:1926–1936.* Dublin, 2002.

Hanley, Brian. *The IRA: A Documentary History, 1916–2005.* Dublin, 2010.

Hayes, Paddy. *Break-out!: famous prison escapes.* Dublin, 2004.

Hopkins, Frank. *Hidden Dublin: Deadbeats, Dossers and Decent Skins.* Dublin, 2008.

Hull, Mark M. *Irish secrets: German espionage in Ireland, 1939-45.* Dublin, 2003.

Kearns, Kevin. *Dublin Pub Life and Lore* Dublin,1996.

Kearns, Kevin. *Dublin Tenement Life* Dublin, 2006.

Krupskaya, Nadezhda. *Memoirs of Lenin.* London, 1970.

Lewis, Jon E. *True World War I Stories.* London, 1997.

Liddy, Pat. *Dublin: A Celebration.* Dublin, 2000.

Liddy, Pat. *Temple Bar: An Illustrated History.* Dublin, 1992.

MacThomáis, Éamonn. *Me Jewel and Darlin' Dublin.* Dublin, 1977

MacThomáis, Shane. *Dead Interesting: Stories from the Graveyards of Dublin.* Dublin, 2011.

Masterson, Larry. *A report on drug abuse in Dublin.* Dublin, 1970.

Matthews, Ann. *Renegades: Irish Republican Women 1900–1922.* Cork, 2010.

Matthews, Ann. *Dissidents: Irish Republican Women 1923–1941.* Cork, 2012.

McCarthy, Cal. *Cumann na mBán and the Irish Revolution.* Cork, 2007.

McCullough, Niall. *Dublin: An Urban History.* Dublin,1989.

McGarry, Fearghal. *Irish Politics and the Spanish Civil War.* Cork, 1999.

McManus, Ruth. *Dublin 1910–1940: Shaping the City and Suburbs.* Dublin, 2002.

Neary, Bernard. *Lugs: The Life and Times of Jim Branigan.* Dublin, 1985.

O'Brien, Joseph V. *Dear, Dirty Dublin: A City in Distress.* Berkeley, 1982.

O'Brien, Mark. *De Valera, Fianna Fáil and the Irish Press.* Dublin, 2001.

O'Brien, Paul. *Blood on the Streets: 1916 & The Battle for Mount Street Bridge.* Dublin, 2008.

O'Connor, Diarmuid. *Sleep Soldier Sleep: The Life and Times of Padraig O'Connor.* Dublin, 2011.

O'Connor, Emmet. *Reds and the Green: Ireland, Russia and the Communist Internationals 1919–43.* Dublin, 2004.

O'Donovan, John. *Life by the Liffey.* Dublin, 1986.

Ó Drisceoil, Donal. *Radical Irish Lives: Peadar O'Donnell.* Cork, 2001.

O'Mahony, Charles. *The Viceroys of Ireland.* London,1912.

O'Reilly, Terence. *Hitler's Irishmen.* Dublin, 2008.

O'Riordan, Michael. *Connolly Column: The Story of the Irishmen Who Fought for the Spanish Republic 1936–1939.* Dublin, 1979.

Prunty, Jacinta. *Dublin Slums 1800–1925.* Dublin, 1998.

Sheehan,Ronan; Walsh,Brendan. *The Heart of the City*. Kerry, 1988.

Stanihurst, Richard. 'Description of Ireland' in *Holinshed's Irish Chronicle 1577*, ed. Liam Miller and Eileen Power. Dublin, 1979.

Stuart, James. *Historical memoirs of the city of Armagh*. Newry, 1819.

Townshend, Charles. *Easter 1916, The Irish Rebellion*. London, 2006.

Yeates, Padraig. *Lockout: Dublin 1913*. Dublin, 2013.

Walker, Joseph Cooper. *Historical Memories of the Irish Bards*. Dublin, 1786.

Walsh, Gerry. *How'ya Doc: The First Ninety Years of the Belvedere Newsboys' Club 1918–2008*. Drogheda, 2010.

Whaley, Thomas. *Buck Whaley's Memoirs: including his journey to Jerusalem*. Dublin, 1906.